Stark Decency

Allen V. Koop

Stark Decency
German Prisoners of War in a New England Village

University Press of New England

Hanover and London

Published by University Press of New England,
One Court Street, Lebanon, NH 03766
www.upne.com

ISBNs for the paperback edition:
    ISBN-13: 978-0-87451-468-1
    ISBN-10: 0-87451-468-1

Printed in the United States of America   10   9

Library of Congress Cataloging-in-Publication Data
    Koop, Allen V., 1944–
        Stark decency.
        Includes bibliographies.
        1. World War, 1939–1945—Prisoners and prisons,
    American. 2. Prisoners of war—New Hampshire—Stark.
    3. Prisoners of war—Germany. 4. Stark (N.H.)—History.
    I. Title.
    D805.U6K57 1988 940.54'72'73097421 88–5550
    ISBN 0–87451–458–4 (cl). ISBN 0–87451–468–1 (pa).
    ∞

to Jennifer and Heather

Contents

Foreword, *ix*

Author's Note, *xi*

1. Introduction, *1*

2. A Place Called Stark, *7*

3. Americans and Prisoners of World War II, *16*

4. The Germans, *28*

5. Strife in a Bitter Place, *40*

6. From Barriers to Bonds, *76*

7. Peace and Despair, *97*

8. Commencement, *108*

9. *Auf Wiedersehen, 115*

   Notes, *124*

   Index, *135*

Illustrations follow page 60.

Foreword

As far as I know there are not many books on German POW camps in the United States of America. Presumably the matter has not proved a magnet to historians because it lacks the elements of high drama: The inmates of those camps were treated correctly, housed and fed properly, and even given a chance to better themselves by acquiring the skills of a trade or an additional education.

True kindness does not advertise itself. Therefore, decent behavior under adverse circumstances, while honored and remembered by the individual beneficiaries, seldom reaches, and rarely leaves a lasting mark on, public consciousness. In writing this book, Allen Koop obviously acted on the impulse of the notion that decency such as that found at Camp Stark should not be forgotten. He tells a tale of implied compassion and of humane values staunchly upheld by a community of simple folk. And we are not allowed to forget the fierce pressures on this haven of unselfconscious goodness from an outside world in turmoil.

We Germans have a long collective memory of war times. We are aware of what it means to be a prisoner of war. We know what it means when the guardians of prisoners forget their own humanity. Even today, more than forty years after the end of World War II, nearly every German family either has a family member or knows somebody who spent some time behind barbed wire as a prisoner of war.

On the chessboard of European history, which has seen so many changes, the Germans figured with varying luck as kings, bishops, or—more often than not—pawns. All age groups of our nation are aware of the suffering we inflicted on our own citizens and later on our neighbors. The education of our people about the horrors perpetrated by Germans during the twelve years from 1933 to 1945 began immediately after the war, when the occupying Allied forces issued licenses to our publishers and broadcasting stations; that process of education has been going on ever since. This continuous education has sharpened our eyes for human suffering wherever it occurs. It has also fortified our minds and alerted our hearts to take a determined stand against any repetition of such suffering. The painstaking examination—especially of our Nazi past—has also brought to light redeeming nuggets, examples of moral courage and decency holding out against crushing odds of baseness and depravity.

This book adds evidential material to the widely held belief in Germany that being a prisoner of war in the United States— *beim Ami,* as the Germans used to phrase it with affectionate respect—amounted to escaping from carnage and iniquity to safety and decency.

Next to the mighty bonds of treaties and multinational business interests, those memories evoked by a receding war may seem fairly humble strands in the sturdy web of shared values that tie Americans and Germans together today. Even so, what happened at Camp Stark deserves to be commemorated in this book. The story of Camp Stark encourages all who will believe that man can be good.

Boston, Massachusetts   HARTMUT LANG, Consulate General
April 1988   of the Federal Republic of Germany

Author's Note

Three phases mark the history of the World War II era. First came the immediate postwar semi-official accounts trumpeting the triumph of the Allies over fascism. Second came a period of sobering investigation, which emphasized the suffering, deceit, and evil on all sides. Recently, a third view has emerged, revealing small sparks of light within the darkness, private moments of goodness. This is the spirit that fostered *Stark Decency*.

The story nearly became lost. It lived, not in files of documents awaiting an historian, but in the remembrance of its participants. History based primarily on interviews requires caution. Unlike documents, interview subjects testify only willingly. Their reasons for wishing to speak out form part of the story. The first few interviews bring more confusion than clarity. Not everyone, I found, remembers Stark the same way. Perspectives differ, opinions clash, memories fail. Yet eventually enough interviews cover sufficiently the full range of perspectives. Finally, the time arrives when additional interviews corroborate, but yield little that is new.

The men and women I interviewed shared with me not only their candid recollections but also their generous hospitality. I am grateful to all of them. Two men requested, for personal reasons, that I allow them to remain anonymous; in the footnotes referring to their testimony I assigned them initials.

Other people in addition to those who participated in the Camp Stark story helped me. Grants from the American Philosophical Society and the New Hampshire Council for the Humanities enabled me to conduct the interviews. My colleagues at Colby-Sawyer College in New London, New Hampshire, served as hosts to my German visitors. Beverly Hurd somehow read my handwriting and typed the manuscript. The people of

Stark were generous, Madeleine magnificent. My mother and father, as always, provided wisdom and encouragement. My daughters lovingly shared me with this book, helping me along the way; I dedicate it to them.

New London, New Hampshire   ·A.V.K.
January 1988

Stark Decency

1

Introduction

June 1944. Mist softened the early morning light at the small military camp twenty miles northwest of Berlin. Inside a row of wooden barracks stretching across a small field carved out of a birch forest, two hundred German soldiers slept fitfully, aware that the Allied invasion of France would determine their fate. At sunrise, they tumbled from their bunks and trudged wearily to the mess hall for breakfast. A day of hard work lay ahead of them. Their muscles still ached from yesterday. Their hands were blistered. They gazed at the world outside, beyond the high fence and four watchtowers that surrounded the camp. This was not an ordinary German military camp but a prison camp. Their guards, however, were not from the S.S. or the Gestapo. They were American soldiers. Nearby Berlin was not the capital of Hitler's Germany, but a paper mill town in the northeastern United States. This was Camp Stark, in the White Mountains, New Hampshire's only World War II prisoner-of-war camp.

The misty start meant a warm day. The bugs would be bad, Albert Lang thought. He waited in the paper company's truck parked outside the camp's main gate. Lang lived just down the road, on the outskirts of the tiny village of Stark. Since boyhood, he had worked in the woods. He had cruised the timber, swung an axe, felled trees, cut cordwood, driven the horses, sharpened the saws. But his job today was something different. Almost two months earlier he had been hired to make woodcutters out of the German prisoners of war. Each day he would drive them along the valley of Mill Brook, then walk them up the hillside to

1

a stand of trees to be felled and then cut to pulpwood length. Sometimes Lang thought the Germans would never get the hang of it. Few of them seemed to care. They worked very slowly. He could not blame them. He probably would work no harder if he were a prisoner in Germany. Some of them struck him as pretty good fellows. He could see that a few of the younger ones enjoyed being outside, working in the woods every day. Albert Lang liked that. He loved the woods. The heavy gate at the entrance to Camp Stark swung open. An Army guard counted the Germans as they filed out, each wearing dark shirts and trousers with "PW" painted in white on the front and back. They climbed into the truck and rode off.

September 1986. It had rained every Saturday all summer, but the first Saturday of autumn sparkled like a jewel. It was going to be one of those fall days in which New Hampshire people take quiet pride. A warm September sun climbed into a cloudless blue sky, quickly banishing the chill from the deep valleys. On the hillsides and up the looming mountains, the hardwood trees blazed red, orange, and yellow. Year to year, the best foliage weekend varies from late September to mid-October. In 1986 it was going to be this weekend, the last in September, Albert Lang thought with satisfaction. He knew the day would bring out the flatlanders, the "leaf-peepers," as natives call the tourists who drive through the mountains, cameras clicking, to record the colorful show that precedes the grey days of late autumn and the blanketing snows of winter. Not that many of them would get this far north. They rarely drove as far as Stark, only thirty miles from the Canadian border.

Albert Lang put on his good suit. He rarely wore a suit, especially on a Saturday afternoon, dressing up only for weddings or funerals. In his seventy-two years, he had attended his share of both. But today was something different. Lang wanted to get there early. He drove into the village and parked on the back side of the bridge, where the honored guests were to meet. He had never seen so many cars in Stark. There must have been more than a thousand people milling around on the far side of the covered bridge, the front side, waiting for things to start. Albert Lang stood a little too stiffly, all dressed up, and shuffled his feet in the dry yellow maple leaves that had already fallen to the ground. He was excited and a little bit nervous. They would arrive soon. Would he recognize any of them? Would they know him?

Most of all, he hoped to see Hermann. All those years ago Hermann and he had spoken—haltingly at first and then more fluently—of the woods and of hunting. Both men loved to hunt. In a day or two, he hoped, after the festivities, they might walk together in the woods, perhaps shooting bear with cameras. But, he told himself, this afternoon was more important. The Germans were coming back. After forty years, some of the Germans were coming back to the village where they had lived as prisoners of war. Albert Lang felt proud to be part of a New Hampshire village and its German soldiers, proud to be part of their unique reunion.

Prisoners of war do not figure as largely in the scholarly or the popular history of World War II as their numbers might warrant. Millions of men were taken captive during the conflict, and their fate touched the lives of millions of families around the globe. The total numbers are difficult to determine, in part because the collapse of Germany and the capitulation of Japan led to the surrender of entire armies and navies. Estimates inflated by these final surrenders run as high as 35 million. Estimates excluding them are said to number some 8 million taken by Germany, 3 million each by Great Britain and by the Soviet Union, and 4 million by the United States.[1] Of the latter, 427,000 were interned on American soil, nearly 372,000 of whom were German soldiers, 50,000 Italian, and 5,000 Japanese prisoners of war.[2] Many Americans have forgotten them. Even more never have known that there were prisoners of war held in the United States. In the collective memory of those years, these prisoners played only a small part.

Historians are often heard to claim that the obscure objects of their research have been "strangely neglected." Usually, such neglect is due to other things having seemed more important at the time. Perhaps they were. Perhaps, too, the prisoner-of-war story was not so much neglected as unready to be told. It took the Camp Stark story nearly four decades to mature before I found it in a village kitchen at the end of a cold, wet October afternoon in 1982.

The seed of interest may have been planted in my mind twenty years earlier when I worked summers caring for climbers' huts in the White Mountains. One of the old-timers said something about there having been a prisoner-of-war camp somewhere up in the North Country during World War II. Did he mention Stark? If so, I may have thought about the camp the day I hitch-hiked through the village on my way to climb the Percy Peaks, but I am not sure. Not until two decades later did it come to mind again. The drive north that October Saturday reminded me that wherever you were, it took a while to get to Stark. I shared the kitchen table and a pot of coffee with an elderly veteran of Camp Stark and his wife.

"Yup," he said, "those were good years for this town. They were the best years I've had. I wouldn't be surprised if some of them German boys felt the same. Yup, we all got along pretty good."

For the historian I had become, that claim about a prison camp aroused equal portions of skepticism and interest. I decided it was worth checking out. Three years later, in another kitchen, this one in a small town in northern Germany, Hermann Osmer confirmed the unexpected assertion, saying, "My imprisonment, my imprisonment in America, was the best time of my life!"

Historians researching World War II prisoner-of-war camps face formidable obstacles. Most of the camps have disappeared, their buildings gone, their sites buried under urban sprawl or reclaimed by nature. Many official documents, especially those pertaining to small camps, have been destroyed.[3] Those that survive are terse; for Camp Stark, the National Archives in Washington, D.C., hold primarily labor reports in summary compilations expressed in man-days of work, offering little insight into life in the camp.

The Camp Stark story had to be sought in the memories of

aging men and women—those not already claimed by death. No roster of the camp's German or American veterans survives. Some of the Americans settled in northern New Hampshire. There, one name led to another, perhaps three or four. As the search widened, despite countless hours consumed combing through German and American telephone books, many suggested names could not be traced. A mobile postwar society had scattered and absorbed numerous American veterans of the camp. Perhaps as many as one-third of the prisoners had returned to homes in East Germany, beyond easy reach today.

Some people preferred not to reopen chapters of life closed so many years earlier. But most of those I managed to contact wanted to talk. They offered their stories helpfully, courteously, and candidly. In the end, the interviews for this book encompassed a variety of people in many places, from Berlin (Germany) to Berlin (New Hampshire), from Maine to Georgia, from Vienna to Vancouver, from the Bavarian Alps to Birmingham, England, from French villages to Austrian foothills. The people who remember Camp Stark form a diverse social group. Not only are they Germans and Americans, but also Austrians and Canadians, English, French, Dutch, and Italians—some of whom have become cosmopolitan world travelers, while others have not strayed far from home. Some seem to remember everything, some have forgotten much. Some are not yet sixty, some nearly ninety. Many were surprised, at first, to encounter interest in the events of nearly forty years before in which they had participated. But even as they spoke, they realized that their private stories were part of something special. Although Camp Stark existed for only two years, its story continues to grow in significance. In the end, Camp Stark changed many people.

Those interviewed told similar stories, but in very different ways. One theme emerged consistently, however. Each person wished to put Camp Stark's best foot forward. It could have gone the other way. Camp Stark, after all, was a prison camp located in a harsh climate. Its people—prisoners, guards, nearby villagers alike—endured discomfort, hardship, strife, anger, fear, sadness, despair. It would have been easy for any of them to talk about the bad times. Some did, but never without returning to a more positive emphasis on the resilience of the human spirit and the manner in which acts of private human decency could prevail over inhumane public policy.

The Americans and Germans at Stark met as enemies, their nations at war with each other. But some of them reached out to find similarities that bound them together. No miracles occurred. No one claimed a new breakthrough in human relations. Whatever good happened did not happen to everyone. Nor did it happen overnight. For some, it took forty years to reach the conclusion that Camp Stark was an island of decency in a world at war.

2

A Place Called Stark

In the first week of April 1944, patches of snow still lingered on the ground. The first train bringing German prisoners of war to Stark was expected to arrive soon at the Percy station. Although Stark was a very small town, in better days it had enjoyed three railroad stations: Stark, Crystal, and Percy. But the depot in the center of the village had closed in 1938, while the tiny Crystal station on the east side of the town lasted only a few years longer. The surviving station, Percy, was the largest of the three; its pivoting water spout gave the Canadian National Railway reason to keep it open.[1] On the station platform the small group of curious and anxious villagers fidgeted while they waited for the train.[2] Around them the natural backdrop of field, forest, and mountain looked the same as it had a generation before, the same as it would a generation hence.

Not much had happened in Stark over the years since it was chartered as Piercy, New Hampshire, in 1774. The town later renamed itself Stark—in honor of John Stark, a New Hampshire Revolutionary War general who never visited the place. It was General Stark who first uttered what in time became the New Hampshire state motto, "Live Free or Die"; ironically, his namesake town would host a prison camp. Most of the homes in Stark were scattered along the banks of the Upper Ammonoosuc River as it twisted its way through the wild northern ranges of the White Mountains.

The mountains of New Hampshire's North Country are not high, only about three thousand feet, but they are steep and rugged. Rocky ledges and sharp cliffs stare out of the dark

7

green fir and spruce forests of their summits. Lower slopes hold the maple, birch, and aspen trees that flame red, orange, and yellow in autumn. The town has never yielded an easy living. In a few places the valley broadens enough to have allowed early settlers to farm rocky but fertile fields along the river, but the steep, forested hillsides and craggy mountains discouraged extensive settlement. Above Stark's weather-beaten, white-painted covered bridge and little white church, the 750-foot dark granite cliff of Devil's Slide forms an imposing, even ominous backdrop for the quiet town.

The pace picked up for a while in the last half of the nineteenth century. When the railroad from Portland to Montreal was hammered through the town in 1852, Stark's boom years began. Sawmills sprang up along the streams. The valleys echoed with the noise of whining saw blades biting into logs harvested in the surrounding woods. Boarding houses filled up with lumberjacks and mill workers. There was a bobbin mill and even a bottling company, which put up Stark Spring Water and a popular orange soda called Howdy Drink.[3] Businesses and people came and went. But by the early twentieth century, they went more than they came. Even before the Great Depression crept northward in the 1930s, Stark had dwindled in size and became increasingly isolated from the outside world. The higher peaks of the White Mountains, including such tourist attractions as Crawford Notch, Franconia Notch, and the Old Man of the Mountains lay to the south. A slender strip of settlement a hundred miles away in Canada was the only civilization standing between Stark and the North Pole. The rail line still linked the village west to the towns of the Connecticut River valley and east to the mill town of Berlin. But except for the daily mail, trains brought little to change the sleepy community.

The image of the isolated Yankee village where time stood still was captured in a 1985 *Boston Globe* feature article. In the 1980s, when much of the rest of New Hampshire was growing at a pace as rapid as any in the nation

> things go on in this town of 470 pretty much as they did a century ago, when the population was about the same . . . Stark is so small it has no town water, no post office, so small that not one town road

is paved from beginning to end. It has a two-room schoolhouse for
six grades, and a library that is open only two hours per week.

The *Globe* quoted a local woman who said, "I would hate to
think things in Stark would ever change."[4] The residents of
Stark viewed their history in terms of people, not events. The
official bicentennial history of the village, published in 1974,
gave most of its coverage to the families of the village rather than
to a chronological narrative. Their personal view of the past and
their remoteness from the world give a special meaning to the
Stark villagers' unexpected and brief experience in international relations in the 1940s.

Neither the Great Depression nor the first three years of the
1940s with the distant war brought much change to Stark. Left
out of the uneven national economic growth during the 1920s,
Stark did not have far to fall in the Depression when hard times
got a little harder, especially for the men who made their living
in the paper mills or in the woods. In a good year the local paper
companies would have over thirty logging camps working
through the winter; in the winter of 1932–33 not one operated.[5]
People accustomed to scraping by just scraped by on a little less.

New Deal measures designed to alleviate the effects of the
Depression tended not to address the economic problems of
Stark. The Civilian Conservation Corps built a work camp on
the Percy plains—a stretch of flat land about two miles up the
river from the covered bridge. The C.C.C. camp's five wooden
barracks, recreation hall, and mess hall were constructed along
the only road running through town, New Hampshire Route
110, which connects Groveton six miles to the northwest with
Berlin twenty-two miles to the southeast. But the camp
remained apart from the people of Stark, for the aim of the
C.C.C. was to assist unemployed urban youth. The young men
imported from New England cities to work on such federal projects as making roads in the White Mountain National Forest
had little impact on the village of Stark. They were there for only
a short while, and before the end of a decade the C.C.C. camp
stood vacant.

World War II also touched Stark lightly at first, bringing

some work, some inconvenience, and some novelty. The resurgent wartime economy opened up jobs in the mill in Berlin and in the woods. Rationed consumer goods led a few inconvenienced people to grumble and others to make secret trips to Canada to fetch commodities unavailable in the United States.[6] The novelty came with Stark's first involvement with the national defense effort. There was concern that the *Luftwaffe* might attempt a sneak attack on New England defense plants, using the Connecticut River valley for navigation. Following government specifications, local citizens erected an aircraft observation post. Electa Osgood went to Portland to receive Air Force instructions in aircraft identification. She returned to recruit observers, often village children, to keep watch around the clock. No enemy planes showed up, but the Stark observers felt they were doing their part.[7]

The outside world knew Stark primarily through postcards and kitchen calendars. The view of its quaint white church and covered bridge set against the dark cliff of spruce-crested Devil's Slide caught the eye of many photographers, but the captions on 1944 calendars that were distributed down country read only "New England Village," preserving both the anonymity and isolation of the town behind the idyllic scene. The few people who lived in Stark, who held pews in that church and strolled across that covered bridge on summer evenings let the rest of the world go by, content to spend their lives in a place of rugged beauty, though days in the deep valley were short, winters long, and icy arctic winds roared down from Canada, penetrating even sturdy clapboard houses. The world—and the war—seemed far away.

The first rumors about the Germans began to buzz around the town early in 1944. Men who worked at the Brown Company paper mill in Berlin heard talk of prisoners of war being assigned to cut pulpwood in the woods to help the company meet its growing wartime production goals. In mid-January men from the U.S. Army and Brown Company officials were observed inspecting the dormant C.C.C. camp. In Percy village, just across the river from the camp, they made inquiries about several vacant houses.[8] In February the rumors were confirmed by a brief article in the local paper, and in March the statewide newspaper announced that a stockade fence and four watchtowers had transformed a former C.C.C. installation into Camp Stark, New Hampshire's sole prisoner-of-war camp.[9] In order to house U.S. military personnel, the Brown Company hastily erected wooden barracks across the road from the camp in a field leased by the army from a local farmer. It all seemed to be happening very quickly and somewhat mysteriously. By mid-March the American soldiers who were to serve as guards had begun to arrive.

Once the camp assumed full operation there were usually between forty and fifty enlisted men, two or three sergeants, a lieutenant or two, a medical officer, and the camp commander in the Camp Stark military unit. These U.S. soldiers were drawn from several sources. Some came from military police battalions in which they had received training in police methods and guard duty. A few other soldiers with no particular training were assigned to guard duty primarily because they were disqualified for a variety of reasons from overseas service. Still others were malaria victims from the Pacific who were ordered to cold-weather stateside posts for health reasons. As time went by, an increasingly large segment of Camp Stark guards were to be combat veterans shipped home from Europe; after the spring of 1945 a few were themselves former prisoners of war in Germany. As in most military units, the American soldiers of Camp Stark reflected widespread geographic distribution and considerable social differentiation. Except for those men who could never cope with a North Country winter, most of the American guards were content at primitive Camp Stark. There were worse places to spend the war. A number had requested this duty in order to be close to their hometowns in northern New England.

The arrival of an army contingent in a village as small as Stark was bound to cause a stir, even before the German prisoners arrived. In Stark, as elsewhere, wartime exigencies accelerated social and cultural change. Local residents began to encounter different kinds of people, and began to think about things in different ways. The young women of the town, as well as those in neighboring Groveton and Berlin, eyed the new young men with interest. Some of the men looked back. A number of American soldiers from Camp Stark married local girls and, after the war, settled down as permanent residents of the area. Church suppers always included the soldiers, greatly enlivening the town's social life. Older folks invited lonely soldiers into their homes for a Sunday meal or a holiday dinner. Evening or weekend passes to Berlin came easily, and local motorists would always pick up servicemen hitch-hiking to or from Camp Stark.[10]

There were, of course, problems from time to time between the townspeople and the soldiers. Usually these stemmed from rowdiness or from traffic accidents. More private but keenly felt on both sides were a number of broken hearts. In general, however, the relationship between the military and the local civilians was cordial and helpful. The spirit of friendly aid to hitchhikers was stretched one day when a serviceman accepted a ride from a carload of women as he walked along the road to the camp. Against regulations, he carried a case of beer on his shoulder. Only when the car arrived at the entrance to the camp did the shocked soldier recognize one of the passengers as the wife of the army doctor and another as the wife of the camp commander. Neither woman breathed a word.[11] A more substantial contribution came from a Groveton woman who provided at her own expense new furniture so the soldiers might enjoy a lounge room at the Spartan army barracks.[12] On the other side, army guards allowed the local school teacher to warm herself in the camp office while she awaited the school bus on frigid mornings. The captain would dispatch an army vehicle to rescue a civilian car that had slithered off the icy road, and medical officer Elliot Foster bent the rules to provide penicillin to local children.[13] Wives and girlfriends of American soldiers were welcomed to the army mess hall where they enjoyed what came to be known as the best food in the North Country.

Three groups of Americans participated in the Camp Stark story. Some American military personnel served at Camp Stark for only a few months or weeks. Some stayed with the camp throughout its tenure, although a few guards were rotated to prisoner-of-war camps in Maine from time to time. The other two groups of Americans, the civilian foremen and the villagers, remained more constant.

The civilian foremen were local men like Albert Lang, hired by the Brown Company to instruct and supervise the German prisoners of war in wood-cutting operations. Many were beyond the age for military service, but were strong, experienced woodsmen, more at home in the deep forests that blanketed the North Country hills than in the towns that dotted the valleys. They knew how to make the forest yield its logs and pulpwood, and they had long ago mastered the tools and elements of their trade: saws, axes, cant hooks, twitch horses, and hard work. They were glad to have work. The 1930s had been years of "tough sleddin' " for such men. Tom Gadwah, for example, was a good man in the saw shop. Few could get an axe or saw blade to hold an edge as well as Tom. But once the cutting and chopping slacked off, there was little for a good saw man to do. When he heard that the army and the Brown Company might need some saws sharpened at the C.C.C. camp they were turning into a prisoner-of-war camp, Tom jumped at the chance.

Many of the foremen hired for Camp Stark came from French-Canadian families. They or their fathers before them had followed the lumber trails from Quebec south into the United States where work had been better in the 1920s. The stream of Quebecois immigrants to the mills and forests of northern New England lent a distinctly French flavor to the region. Saturday morning shoppers browsing on Main Street in Berlin might find themselves in crowds where only French was overheard. The French-Canadians, many of whom still struggled with English, formed a close community. In some small mill towns and in many neighborhoods of larger places the French-Canadians assumed a majority role and set the cultural standards. In the smaller Yankee towns, although assimilated, they formed a French Catholic minority. Still the newcomers, they were not foreigners, but they were not natives. Those who came to work with the German prisoners of war already knew something about cross-cultural communication and cultural alienation.

The third group of Americans who dealt with the Germans of Camp Stark were the villagers themselves. The overtures and responses of ordinary civilians to the Germans were to come slowly, but without the constraints of military discipline or labor policy felt by the soldiers and the camp employees. The local folks' contacts with the Germans may have been fewer, but they were freer. Often the first gestures between Stark villagers and the German prisoners of war involved the wives or children of men who worked at the camp. Then the circle widened gradually to include their relatives and friends. Eventually, over the next forty years, all the people of Stark would come to terms with the relationship between their village and its German prisoners of war.

Of course, not all the Americans, or Germans, of Camp Stark thought deeply about their experience. Some look back on it merely as a time of work to be done, or work to be avoided. One or two elderly Stark residents barely recall the camp. One former foreman interviewed thought primarily in terms of types of trees cut. One or two guards recalled pointless monotony, better at least than being shot at. A few Germans saw those years as part of their life and national history best forgotten. But most of the people at Camp Stark, on both sides of the fence, today realize that they were part of something big, something elusive, something special, possibly for some the most important thing they ever did.

Back at the beginning it was not that clear. On that April day in 1944, the villagers waiting for the arrival of the Germans were simply curious. Some felt anxious, a few downright afraid. Suppose these incoming prisoners were to escape, running through the town, doing harm? One or two people who had already lost a son in battle murmured about Nazis living in their town.[14] But there was no overt hostility. The people of Stark had not learned to hate the enemy. It would take a while, however, before their curiosity and anxiety would change to pity and friendship.

Long before it could be seen, the puffing steam engine could be heard as it chugged along the track from Berlin. A loud whistle signaled the grade crossing just before the special train sighed to a halt at Percy station. Stern-faced armed guards marshaled some one hundred German prisoners dressed in G.I. army clothing out of the coaches. They counted the Germans and then formed them into a column for a half-mile march to the camp. The Germans did not look like Aryan supermen. They looked tired, disheveled, bewildered, and for the most part significantly older than the American soldiers who marched them down the lane, across the bridge, and along the state highway to their new home in the New Hampshire forest.[15]

A few days later, on Easter Sunday, Camp Stark had become something of a local attraction. From near and distant towns motorists arrived, spending rationed gasoline to drive by the camp, gawking at the Germans. The Germans stared back. Some smiled. The American guards firmly ordered the slowing cars along. None was permitted to stop, but a few girls waved.[16]

3

Americans and Prisoners of World War II

German prisoners of war and American civilians were not intended to live close together. They were not supposed to have much to do with each other. Normally prisoner-of-war camps were to be located far away from American communities and highways. But Camp Stark stood astride the only major road in the town, a little more than a mile from the center of the village. The decisions that brought these Germans and Americans close together in Stark were made hundreds, even thousands of miles away.

At the beginning of World War II, the U.S. Government was inexperienced in the prisoner-of-war business. Throughout the history of warfare, prisoners have posed inconvenient dilemmas. In antiquity, belligerents avoided problems by slaughtering their captives or allowing them to starve. In more recent times, Andersonville, Bataan, and Soviet camps—among others—testify that this pattern of savagery has persisted. Continuing brutality defies a series of international agreements designed to regulate prisoner-of-war problems. As early in the national experience as the Revolutionary War the young American goverment negotiated treaties with Great Britain and Prussia concerning English and Hessian captives. The 1785 treaty with Prussia endured to provide the United States and Germany with a framework for prisoner-of-war issues during America's relatively brief participation in World War I.[1] In the optimistic international climate prevailing in the late 1920s, agreements signed in Geneva by forty-seven nations guaranteed that future prisoners of war should receive proper treatment: personal protection, evacuation from combat zones, appropriate food and housing, physical exercise, intellectual diversion, correspondence, and the right to elect spokesmen.[2] These international agreements—the Geneva Convention Relative to the Treatment of Prisoners of War and the Geneva Red Cross Convention—both signed in 1929, assumed the best in the attitude of the captors. (Of course, war itself had been more or less forbidden just the year before with the signing of the Paris Peace Pact.) Any infractions would be investigated by the Swiss and such humanitarian agencies as the International Red Cross Committee and the Y.M.C.A.[3] Behind all the lofty expectations lay the unspoken reality: prisoners of war are hostages. Self-interest compels belligerents not to invite reprisals against its citizens held in enemy hands.

In July 1941, as the United States moved closer to war, President Roosevelt designated Maj. Gen. Allen Gullion as Provost Marshal General to superintend the internment of prisoners of war and enemy aliens. The Provost Marshal General's office did not expect to be overwhelmed. It looked like this was going to be a war fought on battlegrounds thousands of miles from American soil, and at first the only prisoners envisioned were victims of naval conflicts close to American shores. This assumption held during most of 1942. America's first year at war yielded few captives.[4]

Meanwhile, the United States' British ally, at last enjoying military victory in North Africa, became swamped with German prisoners of war. By mid-1942, German defeat in North Africa forced Great Britain to feed and house over a quarter of a million captives. London persistently pressed Washington to help out. At first, the Americans wanted no part of it. Security considerations prompted American reluctance. America's brief and confused experiences with only a thousand German prisoners of war during World War I had left behind a belief, never proven, that escaped prisoners of war somehow were the ones who sabotaged the New Jersey Black Tom munitions plant in 1916.[5] More recently, the arrest and conviction of several German spies in 1942 had raised higher the American concern about security.[6]

Ultimately the logic of the British position prevailed, and the

United States was forced to deal seriously with the prisoner-of-war issue. Initially, the U.S. Government agreed to transport 50,000 German prisoners of war in otherwise empty ships returning to the United States. Very quickly in 1943 the numbers rose to 60,000, then 100,000. By September 1943, over 160,000 German prisoners of war had landed in American ports, and they continued to arrive in even greater numbers.[7]

The rapid surrender of whole armies of German soldiers in the final months of the North African campaign posed logistical problems for the Allied captors. The under-staffed American prisoner-of-war enterprise held a low priority in the larger war effort. At first, the confused Americans did not seem to know quite what to do with so many captives—who themselves were even more confused. Surrender and rapid evacuation from combat produce a strange psychological shock, rendering most captives completely docile.[8] Normally soldiers spend little time anticipating surrender, but German troops seemed especially unprepared for the prospect of capture.[9] Passivity tends to be reinforced in the new prisoner of war by the disappearance of his comrades and by a keen awareness of the power of the enemy. After a few days the prisoner of war begins to regain his bearings, although driven to irritability and despair at the prospect of incarceration in close quarters.[10] He possesses an outlook differing from that of a criminal prisoner. Although both are held captive, the prisoner of war, unlike the criminal, has done nothing "wrong." He has committed no crime against society and usually bears no stigma. The criminal prisoner, however, at least knows how long his incarceration will last, while the prisoner of war never knows when or even if he will be liberated.

Once Washington agreed to house German prisoners of war on American soil, they were moved along as rapidly as westbound shipping became available. Afrika Korps captives were packed in steamy railroad freight cars enroute to Algerian ports. Later in the war, German troops captured in France took a seasick journey across the English Channel in creaking landing craft before they were entrained to a port of embarkation, usually Liverpool. These uncomfortable and cramped journeys served to increase Germans' anxiety about their treatment in captivity, especially when civilians in French North Africa and England would spit and hurl insults at them.[11]

The major concern during the trans-Atlantic crossing was attack by German submarines. Although from time to time the Americans sounded a U-boat alarm, no ship carrying German prisoners of war was ever sunk.[12] Seasickness, stale air, cramped quarters, and boredom marked the voyage—the same conditions faced by American G.I.s sailing in the opposite direction.[13] Slow ships and stormy weather could stretch the voyage to two weeks, although some German prisoners of war, including a few who came to Camp Stark, were whisked across in fewer than six days on the *Queen Mary*.[14] Arrival in an American port, usually New York, Norfolk, or Boston, brought exclamations of surprise and wonder. Before their capture, many German soldiers had been told that New York and other American coastal cities had been leveled by the *Luftwaffe*, and that the Statue of Liberty had been destroyed.[15] The sight of an undamaged metropolis, a bustling harbor, and civilian cars racing along the highways attested to the strength of the wartime American economy, although some Afrika Korps captives concluded that it was all staged to impress them, the German soldiers who were certain to welcome *der Führer* when he arrived to conquer America.[16]

Preconceived Nazi stereotypes of undisciplined and corrupt Americans often seemed confirmed by initial contacts with the American soldiers who processed the German prisoners of war at the ports of disembarkation. German-speaking American soldiers were scarce, most having been assigned to intelligence units. It was not uncommon for arriving prisoners of war to be examined and interrogated by a refugee German doctor who failed to disguise his contempt and antipathy.[17] The informal, democratic American army in which officers joked with enlisted men made no sense to the Germans.[18] The American soldier assigned to guard the newly arrived Germans held a low priority job, and he knew it. This was probably as close as he would get to the real war, so he viewed the prisoners of war as a source of souvenirs: medals, decorations, daggers, etc. But these backwater soldiers who pilfered Nazi memorabilia exercised their armed authority, and they often menaced the Germans as they herded them to the trains that would carry them to prison camps.[19]

At the railroad station, the prisoners of war received another shock—this one more positive. Accustomed to being transported in German boxcars, they were amazed to settle into the upholstered seats of American passenger coaches. As the trains rolled along endless miles of the American landscape the Germans gazed at the breadth, beauty, and wealth, mixed with the desolation and poverty of this contradictory country.[20] The first prisoner-of-war trains tended to head south or southwest. The security-conscious office of the Provost Marshal General wanted to keep prisoner-of-war stockades in places like Texas and Oklahoma, far from defense plants on the East and West Coasts, and where mild climates lowered maintenance costs.[21] But abandoned Civilian Conservation Corps camps and unused areas of military bases filled up rapidly, compelling the U.S. Government to relax its geographic limitations on prisoner-of-war camps. Eventually almost 400,000 German prisoners of war would occupy over 500 camps located in almost every state.[22] In some places entire new camps had to be built, the government taking care to construct these to the same standards as American military bases, in strict compliance with the letter of the Geneva Convention.[23]

At times the War Department's adherence to the terms of the Geneva Convention raised the ire of the American people. Repeatedly, local grumblers, hometown newspapers, and even the national press accused the government of "coddling" the German prisoners of war. It may have been difficult to reach agreement on what "coddling" really meant, but no one doubted that the prisoners of war were treated well. Usually, their basic standard of living—food, housing, sanitation, recreation—reached a higher level inside their American stockades than in the German army. American commitment to uphold the Geneva Convention extended to granting permission for the Germans to wear Nazi uniforms, decorate barracks with swastika flags, use the Hitler salute, and even, in some cases, celebrate Nazi holidays.[24]

There were two reasons for the generous treatment the United States afforded its German prisoners of war. First and most important was the assumption, or perhaps the hope, that proper treatment of German prisoners of war in America would win similar treatment for American prisoners in German hands. Humanitarian agencies like the International Red Cross made frequent inspections of prisoner-of-war camps on both sides, and reported to each government on the conditions under which its soldiers were held prisoner. The U.S. Government decided the best service it could render to captive Americans was to give the Nazi regime no excuse for reprisal, and to provide an example of proper treatment of prisoners of war. The second objective was to save American lives by shortening the conflict through encouraging massive German surrender. It was assumed that widespread knowledge of benevolent American treatment of prisoners of war, plus General Eisenhower's "safe conduct passes" dropped over German positions, would prompt the Germans to choose surrender rather than prolonged combat.

An evaluation of the success of these two objectives of American prisoner of war policy remains difficult. Toward the end of the war in Europe, German soldiers did surrender to Americans in droves, possibly because of the simply overwhelming American combat effectiveness and the total collapse of the Nazi military machine. But there is evidence that American prisoner-of-war policy also played a role. Certainly the German soldiers tumbled over themselves to surrender to American forces rather than to the Red Army. The Soviet Union had not signed the Geneva Convention and made no pretense of proper treatment for its German prisoners of war. There is thus compelling evidence that propaganda about American prisoner-of-war policy played a significant role in effecting the surrender of German military units, although few observers would hazard a quantitative judgment on this.[25]

As far as achieving better treatment for American captives in Germany is concerned, the War Department's prisoner-of-war policy earned a mixed judgment. There is no doubt that German prisoners of war in the United States fared much better than did Americans in Germany. There is no doubt that many, perhaps most, American prisoners in Germany suffered terrible privation. When camps holding American prisoners of war were liberated in the spring of 1945, the American people expressed outrage at the conditions under which captive G.I.s had existed.[26] Public opinion in America was enflamed by descriptions of starving G.I.s who lost over 100 pounds subsisting on grass soup at *Stalags* at Bad Orb, while many of their fellow captives died.[27] As terrible as the conditions were, however, many observers and even some victims claimed the starvation rations reflected the collapse of the German economy more than malevolent Nazi policy.[28] Postwar investigations concluded that the German government tried at times to meet provisions of the Geneva Convention.[29] Although reports of mistreatment persisted, the general conclusion which emerged was that American prisoners of war in Germany at least suffered less because of the example of American compliance with the letter and spirit of the Geneva Convention. The Nazis displayed sinister differentiation among their various types of prisoners. Maltreated as some American prisoners of war may have been, they nonetheless fared better than most other victims of Nazi incarceration and extermination.

These finer points of argument, however, could be lost when the American public became disturbed about "coddling" German prisoners of war. The U.S. Government worked to create a sense of national unity in the civilian war effort by churning up emotions, but at the same time its officials wanted the public to consider their prisoner-of-war policy with cool detachment and calm logic.

Concerns about coddling appeared in the press almost as soon as the first prisoners of war arrived.[30] The simple notion that these Germans should breathe pure American air while American boys were shipped overseas to fight Nazism was enough to enrange some American citizens. The man who suggested, "Put them in Death Valley, chuck in a side of beef, and let them starve to death," no doubt expressed the visceral reaction of many.[31] However, the articles that appeared in 1943 and 1944 in periodicals like *Collier's* and *American Magazine* always reached the same conclusion: Yes, the German prisoners of war in the United States are treated well, perhaps better than they deserve; no, they are not being "coddled" or "pampered." The articles sought to reassure the American public of the wisdom of the War Department's prisoner-of-war policy, which was concerned above all else with the fate of American captives in Germany.[32] In 1945 the coddling question heated up again over the issue of food. Although food rationing and food shortages in the United States were trivial inconveniences compared to the human suffering in other nations during World War II, the American public became annoyed by rumors that German prisoners of war were eating better than patriotic civilians. A congressman visiting a prisoner-of-war camp in Arizona reported that the Germans were "as fat as hogs."[33] The furor died down, but only after a series of articles and pronouncements that the Geneva Convention stipulated a diet for prisoners of war similar to that of the military personnel of the captor. The United States was bound to respect the Geneva Convention.

For a number of reasons, coddling never became a major issue at Stark, although the camp commander followed army policy by speaking once in a while to fraternal organizations or business groups in surrounding towns to allay concern, especially on the subject of food. Having good food or, sometimes, enough food was a problem for some Stark families even in peacetime. When the local pig farmer who collected the garbage at Camp Stark began to tell how he found the uncooked Christmas turkey right on top of the pail, it led to talk. Later some people realized that the Germans probably had never before confronted a turkey dinner, and might not have known what they were missing.[34] Eventually the coddling issued faded at Stark and elsewhere simply because the German prisoners of war had made themselves useful to the Americans.

The magnitude of the military and industrial demands of World War II surpassed the resources of each major belligerent. Each needed more men for its army. Each demanded more laborers for its work force. Each held enemy prisoners of war. The solution became obvious. In Germany the great demand for prisoner-of-war labor led Hitler to compromise the application of his racial theories to labor policy. At first Slav prisoners had been deemed unworthy even to work as laborers for the Third Reich. But then the demands for coal outweighed notions of racial purity, and Soviet prisoners of war were ordered to work in German coal mines. Captured Soviet partisans, at first liable to be shot, were instead shipped to German mines. The Soviet Union made similar use of German prisoners of war.[35] In the United States the decision to employ prisoners of war came in a slow and complicated way.

Americans had employed prisoners of war, or at least considered doing so, in national conflicts since the Revolutionary War. But the most immediate precedent, World War I, offered little guidance. In that war the Americans held only 1,346 enemy prisoners of war, and the idea of employing them produced more planning than labor.[36] The Geneva Convention permitted prisoners of war to labor for their captors, and it devoted many of its articles to that subject. There were several general guidelines. Enlisted men could be required to work; officers could refuse. Workers had to be paid, either in currency or scrip. Laborers had to be physically fit, and not employed in dangerous work or in work directly related to war operations. Interpretation of these guidelines was not always clear, especially when it came to determining what was meant by labor directly related to war operations or what constituted dangerous work. Eventually, always considering the possible impact of its decisions on American prisoners of war in Germany, the War Department decided that anything not specifically forbidden was allowed.[37] At first prisoner-of-war labor was intended only on secure military bases where prisoners could perform menial and clerical jobs in order to free American soldiers for combat. But very quickly it became clear that the greater demand lay in the private sector. The need was greatest in agriculture because farmers all across the country were forced to plow under ripe crops left unharvested for want of agricultural laborers.[38]

Typically, the simple decision to make prisoner-of-war labor available on a contract basis to civilian employers produced a web of complicated regulations. The War Department and the War Manpower Commission came to an agreement in July 1943 that protected the Geneva Convention rights of the prisoners of war and also required that prisoner-of-war labor not compete with civilian labor.[39] Prisoner-of-war laborers were to be paid 80 cents per day with the possibility of earning as much as $1.50 per day under incentive plans. Payment was to be in scrip, which could be used in the camp canteen or placed in a savings account to be released after repatriation. Contractors were to pay the government the going local rate for labor, the difference used to defray the expenses of the prisoner-of-war program.[40]

The decision to allocate prisoner-of-war labor throughout the forty-eight states led to a change in incarceration policy. It was impractical to transport workers many miles to the work sites from existing prisoner-of-war camps, which housed between seven thousand and twelve thousand men. Therefore, the prisoner-of-war laborers were distributed to a network of over five hundred small branch camps scattered across the land from the Wyoming prairies, to Mississippi cotton country, to New York orchards—even to the northern woods of New Hampshire.

One harvesting operation and industry severely crippled by the labor shortage was the pulpwood industry. Times had changed quickly for loggers. The idle years of the Depression had given way during the war to plenty of work. Better still, easier work and higher wages beckoned in defense plants far from the forest. Pulpwood states found themselves in need of thousands of loggers.[41] Since the pulpwood and paper products industries produced a host of items essential to the war effort, the government moved quickly toward using prisoners of war to cut pulpwood. Immediately, it ran into three problems. First, some preliminary experiments indicated that prisoners of war were not readily transformed into effective woodsmen; even with increased supervision and instruction they produced only a fraction of the daily cut produced by free labor. Second, American labor, in the form of the International Woodworkers of America, protested vehemently against being undercut by German prisoners of war.[42] Finally, the War Department had determined earlier that felling trees with sharp instruments was a form of dangerous work forbidden by the Geneva Convention. The continued shortage led the government to change its mind. It suddenly decided that cutting smaller pulpwood trees was not all that dangerous. Labor union objections were more or less ignored, and the War Production Board concluded that some pulpwood was better than none.[43] German prisoners of war were taken to the forests. Army guards went along, to keep prisoners from literally taking to the woods.

Because the higher-paying defense plants were close enough to lure laborers down country, pulpwood companies in the Northeast were among the hardest hit by the workers' flight from the forest. Northern New Hampshire's largest paper company in particular needed help. In July 1943, the Brown Company of Berlin, New Hampshire, opened negotiations with the federal government in order to obtain prisoners of war to cut pulpwood.

Berlin, with a population of 20,000, was easily the largest town in northern New Hampshire, enjoying a setting as majestic as any in New England. At the foot of the Presidential Range, highest in New England, with rugged peaks snow-covered nearly six months of the year, the town climbed steep hillsides along the banks of the broad Androscoggin River. Outside the town, forested hills and jewel-like lakes stretched toward Maine, Canada, and Vermont. Yet Berlin itself, despite its beautiful location, was not a pretty place. Upstream from the dam at the paper mill the river was clogged for miles with floating pulpwood. Downstream it gurgled with industrial pollution, its banks collecting debris and foam. Except for a few graceful neighborhoods, it was a work-worn place of wooden apartment buildings, run-down houses, and an undistinguished commercial center. As in most paper towns, a malodorous, acrid, sulfurous cloud hung over its buildings most days. Berliners had become a close family, however, a loyal, hard-working, and largely French-Canadian population. Most people in the northern third of the state knew that their prospects and fortunes were tied to Berlin's. It was a company town, and the company was the Brown Company. What was good for the Brown Company was good for the region.

In a normal year, the company employed some two thousand woodcutters; in 1943 the number had dwindled to little more than one thousand. Local newspapers called attention to New Hampshire's failure to meet forty percent of its War Production Board quota of pulpwood.[44] The company already had its eye on the closed C.C.C. camp outside Stark village as a place to house the prisoner-of-war laborers. New Hampshire politicians Sherman Adams and U.S. Senator Styles Bridges intervened to help steer the Brown Company's proposal through the War

Manpower Commission. It became a complicated task. After officially ascertaining the need for woodcutters, the unavailability of local civilian labor, the price to be paid for the wood, the conditions under which the prisoners of war would work, the suitability of housing for civilian and military personnel, and still other responsibilities of the Brown Company and the U.S. Government, the company submitted its application and eventually won approval.[45]

The entire process from the time the idea of using prisoners of war for woodcutters was first broached until they actually arrived consumed over ten months. The nearest source of such labor was 250 miles distant—the German prisoner-of-war compound attached to the U.S. Army base at Fort Devens, near Ayer, Massachusetts. But Fort Devens was an unusual German prisoner-of-war camp. Fort Devens was an anti-Nazi camp.

4

The Germans

At the outset of their participation in World War II, most Americans, including those administering the prisoner-of-war program, had little idea how to regard and treat anti-Nazi German soldiers. Official wartime propagandists attempted to make clear that the enemy was fascism or Nazism or militarism, but in everyday parlance it was simply easier for Americans to talk about fighting the Germans and the Japanese. The United States was the only major belligerent whose civilian population remained unscathed by combat, and there were times when some complacent citizens seemed to need reminding: "Don't you know there's a war on?" In this situation, government war information agencies' continuing efforts to clarify the basic issues of the protracted conflict, by asking Americans to discern political differences within the populations of its adversaries, tended to complicate the task of focusing the national war effort. Camp Stark reflected the resultant confusion.

Yet, World War II was very much a political struggle, and the American war objectives were political as well as military. Although intended to be complementary, in the prisoner-of-war program these objectives came into conflict with each other. The U.S. Government's primary wartime concern—to win the war as rapidly as possible while losing as few American lives as possible—dictated almost every one of its decisions, from tactical plans to inter-allied strategy to dealing (or not dealing) with postwar considerations. However, the United States committed itself not only to defeating fascism but also to replacing this political philosophy with democratic governments fostering political, social, and economic values similar to those of most Americans. The political objective sustained the military objective, providing it with the moral strength of a crusade.

To achieve its political objective the United States needed to identify, distinguish, and support anti-Nazi elements within the German nation and the German army—an effort that would take time, discernment, and manpower. Although the American authorities realized early that anti-Nazis formed part of the German prisoner-of-war population, almost no steps were taken initially either to accommodate or make use of them. To achieve its purely military objective, Washington required the prisoner-of-war program to operate on the lowest possible investment of manpower. As a result of its initial decision to subordinate the prisoner-of-war program to the military objective rather than utilize it to further the political objective, the War Department almost lost control of the program—and allowed the creation of perhaps hundreds of Nazi enclaves within the United States.

The official disinclination to confront political tensions among the German prisoners of war and the consequent slowness with which Nazis were segregated from anti-Nazis reflected the low priority assigned to enemy prisoners within the American war plan. Choosing to administer the prisoner-of-war program with minimal and often underqualified personnel may have aided the speedy prosecution of America's overseas military effort, but it undermined the aim of replacing fascism in Germany with an anti-fascist democratic society. The shortage of properly trained U.S. Army personnel in the prisoner-of-war program created many long-term problems, critical both at the time of capture and later in the administration of the large base camps.

The disorientation experienced by almost any captive at the moment he is taken prisoner makes this the best time for his captor to extract military intelligence, political beliefs, or personal information. But American authorities wasted little time or effort on new captives. Once a German soldier was captured, he had no further military significance and needed only to be evacuated from the combat zone. The relatively few American soldiers assigned to initial contact with newly captured Germans received no instruction about political issues. They were ordered only to make the easiest separation decisions: air force personnel were removed from army, officers from enlisted men. No attempt was made to segregate anti-Nazis.[1]

Content to maintain order, the Americans rarely intervened in relationships between Germans. By the time the German prisoners of war finally reached the United States their own military command order had generally reasserted itself. The moment of arrival at major prisoner-of-war camps often provided dedicated Nazi prisoners of war with their best opportunity to assume control. The scarcity of German-speaking American military personnel in the United States led camp commanders responsible for as many as 5,000 prisoners or more to rely upon English-speaking prisoners, whatever their beliefs. The Americans wanted their prisoner-of-war camps to operate smoothly, even if that meant allowing ardent Nazis to run German affairs inside the camps. When life in the camps failed to run smoothly, the problems, which usually stemmed from the struggles of anti-Nazi prisoners of war to avoid the harsh domination of the Nazis who controlled them, led the American authorities to associate the anti-Nazis with disorder. Order became more important than individual rights. From the beginning, American commanders and guards tended to brand anti-Nazis as trouble-makers.[2]

Even if the Americans had attempted seriously to fathom the relationships among National Socialism, Hitler, and the German nation, they might have found themselves on a different wavelength from the German prisoners of war, anti-Nazis and Nazis alike. For the Americans, National Socialism meant a malignant political philosophy, which expressed itself in militarism, persecution, oppression, conquest, and sadistic cruelty. Hitler was the personification of this evil force. Most Germans, they thought, probably went along with National Socialism, and certainly most captured German soldiers seemed to be Nazis. Therefore it made sense to treat them all the same.

However, Allied surveys of German prisoner-of-war attitudes conducted near the conclusion of the war revealed a greatly different German perspective. Most Germans saw Hitler more as a personal leader, *der Führer,* than as an ideological leader. They could separate the man from the Nazi regime and even from the philosophy. In the face of impending military defeat, German confidence in Hitler remained very high until the last months of the war. He remained about the fray, above the problems, as the psychological leader of the people. Failure, reversal, disappointment were considered to be the fault of his subordinates, while Hitler escaped blame.[3] Allegiance to Hitler was not, however, necessarily tantamount to embracing the creed of National Socialism.[4] While Americans identified Nazism with its methods of oppression, the surveyed prisoners of war stressed its economic and social accomplishments. Many of them admired National Socialism for achieving its "democratic" goals, meaning the way in which Nazi policies accomplished social leveling and economic stability.[5] Even when surveyed prisoners expressed frustration or dissatisfaction with the fascist means employed, they nonetheless admired these social and economic goals.[6] Some postwar surveys did nonetheless reflect considerable variability among German prisoner-of-war respondents concerning their degree of approval of a number of specific National Socialist tenets. American prisoner-of-war officials grasped few of these different ways of looking at issues, which to them seemed simple.

The relationships among National Socialism, the German army, and, ultimately, the prisoner of war himself played a role in shaping these opinions that was as much social as ideological. Although the German army was able to keep its distance from the Nazi party in the early years of the Hitler regime, and was able to avoid complete institutional identification with Nazism until 1944, nonetheless National Socialism played a major role in army cohesion through its domination of the group ethos. For German soldiers, it was common for group solidarity within the small military unit to be achieved through the fusion of patriotism and National Socialism. The individual soldier's acceptance by the group assumed a dimension of political nationalism. Subsequent studies revealed the importance of group identity and solidarity rather than ideology or externally focused political loyalty in maintaining cohesion in the German army even during the military defeat.[7] After capture it was the reconstituted relationship between the individual prisoner of war and his immediate social group that allowed the Nazi hierarchy in the camp to achieve and maintain control. The strength of National Socialism as a social force as well as a political ideology made it difficult and even dangerous for anti-Nazi prisoners of war to assert or even identify themselves.

The array of forces standing against the anti-Nazi were sufficiently intimidating to prompt American researchers after the war to conduct a series of studies on shared traits of anti-Nazi German prisoners of war in order to determine what would prompt a man to become an active anti-Nazi. Two consistent factors proved to be age and a personal history of strong political conviction. All surveys agreed that men over the age of 30, men who had personal and social roots in an ethic antedating Nazism, were those most likely to be anti-Nazis.[8] Immediate postwar case studies of anti-Nazis attempted to stress the role of deeply embedded political belief, usually socialist or communist, often passed down from father to son. "We have always been Social Democrats!" seemed sufficient answer to a researcher's question about specific examples of anti-Nazi activity. When common anti-Nazi personality traits were sought, terms like self-assurance, courage and obstinacy appeared frequently.[9] But personality assessment of prisoners of war yielded vague results. Attempts at a political census of German prisoners of war proved unreliable. Estimates of the percentage of Nazis in American prisoner-of-war camps stretched in early guesses from 6 to 90 percent. More thorough studies conducted toward the end of the war suggested a figure of forty percent pro-Nazi prisoners of war, although the degree of dedication could not be ascertained.[10]

Whatever the percentages, it is clear that there were significant numbers of anti-Nazi prisoners of war, and it is certain that the political struggles between Nazi and anti-Nazi German prisoners of war led to violence in the camps. Anti-Nazis, or even those prisoners of war who wished to remain apolitical, found themselves in jeopardy from the moment of their arrival in most American camps. The seniority system among prisoners of war encouraged Nazi control. Usually the first prisoners to arrive in a major camp were Afrika Korps veterans seized early in the North African campaign. These men tended to preserve their confidence and even arrogance because their capture came before eventual German defeat began to appear inevitable. They were the men who seized control of the patterns of power inside the camp, and they continually extended their authority over newcomers.[11] The fanatic Nazis among them moved to control the behavior and thought of the other prisoners. They censored American newspapers and magazines before permitting other prisoners to read them, snipping out any references to American power or German weakness. The Nazi prisoner-of-war leaders were surprisingly successful in persuading the others that the apparent prosperity and power of the United States were the result of staged efforts to impress the German prisoners of war who would some day soon be ruling the Americans.[12] If persuasion or peer pressure failed to achieve Nazi control, intimidation could succeed. The most common examples, usually believed, threatened reprisals against the prisoner's family back in Germany or against himself after the war.[13] The average prisoner of war had little trouble believing that somehow the Gestapo knew about what happened in prisoner-of-war camps in the United States. For a short time, Nazi activists were able to infiltrate an American censorship and routing office for German prisoner-of-war mail.[14] Ultimately, prisoners of war who cooperated with the Americans or who for any reason were deemed insufficiently dedicated to Nazism could find themselves hauled before a Nazi kangaroo court. Anti-Nazis became victims of savage beatings. Sometimes they were given broken bottles or razor blades to facilitate forced suicide. Sometimes they were simply murdered.[15] The number of German prisoners of war who died in the violent political conflict within the camps is uncertain. American officials set the figure unrealistically low, under six; a French study stretched the estimate to 167.[16]

By early 1944, the American public began to get wind of the scandalous situation inside Nazi-dominated prisoner-of-war camps. Press accounts accused camp commanders of insensitivity toward democratic or anti-Nazi prisoners.[17] The War Department's response to the political problems inside the camps came with glacial speed and inappropriate procedures. The first attempt to segregate anti-Nazis from Nazis was foolishly ill-advised. Anti-Nazis who sought to be removed from their Nazi-dominated environment were asked to come forward. This meant that they were forced to identify themselves without receiving any guarantee that the Americans could protect them or their families against later Nazi reprisal. Not surprisingly, this method produced relatively few anti-Nazis, erroneously confirming the conviction that most German prisoners of war were Nazis.[18] Eventually, it took the intervention of Mrs. Eleanor Roosevelt to adjust government policy to favor the anti-Nazis rather than the Nazis. After a White House tea at which the First Lady learned the dimensions of the problem she exclaimed, "I've got to talk to Franklin. Right in our backyard, to have these Nazis move in and controlling the whole thought process! What do you think this does to us?"[19]

Soon after, the American army reviewed its order of segregation, first identifying and removing the most obdurate hardcore Nazis, and then selecting the anti-Nazis, especially those who claimed to be in physical danger. By 1945 over 4,500 of the most visible Nazis had been shipped to a special camp at Alva, Oklahoma.[20] The number fell far short of the size of the avowed Nazi prisoner population, testifying to the continued inadequacy of the army's political segregation program. A similarly small number of dedicated anti-Nazis was split between Camp Campbell, Kentucky, and Fort Devens, Massachusetts.

Among the early arrivals at Fort Devens were men from the most unusual unit in the Germany army, the 999th Division, and it was men from the 999 who were to form the majority of Camp Stark's prisoner-of-war population, lending the camp its singular character. A controversial decision by Adolf Hitler had started them down the road that in time would take them to Stark.

By 1942 the war had lasted too long for Germany. No matter how bloated by recent conquests, Germany was still a relatively small power locked in combat with industrial giants. *Blitzkrieg* had been the strategy devised to enable a small and only recently armed power to achieve those rapid victories which it might be denied in a long war. *Blitzkrieg* worked in 1939 and 1940 as German armies flashed to lightning victories in Poland, Scandinavia, and Western Europe. But 1941 brought a different result. The inability of the Wehrmacht to defeat the Red Army in the summer of 1941 and the American entry into the war at the end of that year meant that the Germans would have to fight a long war. And by 1942 they had begun to run out of soldiers. However, there was a group of able-bodied men in the Third Reich whom the Wehrmacht had passed by: men then in prison and others whose recent imprisonment had made them undesirable to the Wehrmacht. Ignoring the vehement protests of his officer corps, Hitler secretly ordered the formation of a special penal unit *(Strafbataillon)* composed of men released from prisons: the 999th Penal Division.[21]

This strange outfit was kept isolated from the rest of the German army, gathering in October 1942 at Heuberg, an isolated plateau with forested hills south of Stuttgart. The new recruits were older and less physically fit than those reporting to normal induction centers in Germany.[22] Each had problems in his past. Some of the men who formed the 999 were true criminals: cutthroats, rapists, thieves.[23] However, most of these new soldiers were political offenders, primarily Social Democrats and members of the German Communist Party whose political activities had run them afoul of the Nazi authorities. For example, of those who eventually went to Stark, one had been arrested for distributing Social Democrat literature in the Sudetenland, another had served as an editor of a small socialist newspaper, while another had aroused Nazi ire as an outspoken socialist delegate in his *Landtag*. These political activities had earned them terms of between two and eight years in prison or concentration camps. Another group in the 999 found themselves training at Heuberg after a more circuitous journey. In the late 1930s some German leftists had broken overtly with most of their countrymen over the issues in the Spanish Civil War. These men had volunteered to fight in communist brigades on the republican side in the Spanish Civil War. Their cause was doomed, due in part to the assistance rendered to Franco by Hitler's Germany, and after the Franco victory these German leftists had escaped over the Pyrenees, joining the stream of refugees flowing into France. Interned in camps in southern France, they fell into Nazi hands after Germany defeated France and joined the other members of the 999 who were given the chance to redeem themselves through military service to the Third Reich.[24]

Although the rest of the German army regarded the 999 with disdain for its motley membership, many of the political prisoners wore their assignment to the 999 as a badge of honor.[25] They were proud to be recognized as political dissidents, and they made the most of the opportunity to discuss their plans with those who shared their politics, plans that did not envision dying for Hitler's Germany.[26] After initial training at Heuberg, the 999 encamped in Belgium, where, a decidedly odd occupying army unit, they were surprised and pleased to find themselves warmly received by some Belgians because the clandestine press had made known their unusual political heritage. After a number of the newly arrived anti-fascist soldiers made contact with local Belgian resistance groups, the German authorities moved them once again.

Meanwhile Hitler decided to rename the unit, designating it as Afrika Division 999. This was Nazi military weakness masquerading as strength. The 999 was never close to division capacity and was poorly supplied with weapons, uniforms, and food.[27] Nevertheless, in March 1943, as the military situation in North Africa deteriorated for the Germans, African Division 999 was hurried through Marseilles and Sicily to Tunisia, where they found Field Marshal Rommel's forces in trouble before the advancing American and British armies.[28] But the 999 was in no shape for serious combat. The penal unit lacked the solidarity required for effective fighting. The political and criminal elements never meshed, and their officers were embarrassed to be associated with them and even afraid to entrust their lives to the company of such fellow soldiers, deemed untrustworthy by society.[29] Notwithstanding, in early April military necessity threw the new arrivals into combat in the Kairouan-Pichon area.

The men of the 999 knew they were being *"verheizt,"* used as kindling wood.[30] While some soldiers of the 999 may have fought with tenacity, especially criminals seeking to win their way back into Germany society, most sought surrender. Their units lacked the group cohesion required to sustain combat in the teeth of the relentless Anglo-American assault.[31] Many of the former political prisoners in the 999 shared the political ideology of their enemies rather than the Nazi beliefs of their compatriots. Being strafed by German aircraft did little to keep them fighting.[32] These men left their units as soon as possible, running forward toward the enemy. They hid in sweltering burned-out Panzer tanks, and wandered along the wadis at night until encountering an American patrol to whom they could surrender.[33] The 999 division disintegrated, a part of one of the largest surrenders in military history, as over 150,000 men of Rommel's armies were taken prisoner.

The men of the 999 waited their turn to make the long journey from a desert holding pen to a prisoner-of-war camp in the United States. By the time they arrived to be processed in their first large base camp in the United States, the War Department had begun the initial phase of its political segregation plan. The 999 stood out as a unique military unit, allowing its members to be identified easily as anti-Nazis, so they were tagged for the main anti-Nazi camp at Fort Devens.

By the spring of 1944, the Fort Devens prisoner-of-war camp was filling rapidly with over two thousand Germans already there and more on the way.[34] The men lived in close quarters, their days filled with monotonous labor in Quartermaster Corps warehouses alternating with hours of regimented idleness. Many hoped for a better assignment. When a detachment of the 999 quartered there heard a call for volunteers to go to a woodcutting camp in the north, some thought it sounded better than life at crowded Fort Devens. The description of the outdoor work made it seem invigorating, and they were told that they would enjoy more freedom at the smaller branch camp.[35] Not quite enough volunteered, so the army selected a few others to round out the company of about 100 men chosen to open Camp Stark.

Early on a cool April morning they climbed aboard their northbound train. The men of the 999 had seen their share of trains in the last year and a half. First, from prison to Heuberg, to Belgium, to Marseilles, to Sicily. It was almost exactly one year since many of them had picked their way across North African battlefields to surrender. Then there had been more trains, from Tunisia to Casablanca, from New York to Mississippi, back through New York to Boston, to Fort Devens. Now the company from the 999 chugged through the New England countryside. As they gained miles, they seemed to go back in time. The barely green fields of Massachusetts gave way to still brown fields and snowy mountains. It was mud season, that awkward New Hampshire transition from winter to spring. A stir of excitement rippled through the coach as the train passed by the station clearly marked "Berlin." Less than an hour later they came to a halt at the Percy station in the village of Stark. The Germans climbed off the train, and looked around, thinking they had stopped in the middle of nowhere.[36]

Their first impressions of Stark were to last. It seemed remote and ruggedly scenic—words Stark villagers would themselves use to describe their town. For a few German city dwellers who had never left Cologne, Essen, or Hamburg until their induction into the German army, it was but one more desolate place, like Heuberg or Tunisia, to which their military service had sent them. To others, especially those from Bavaria or Austria, it was more like home than any place they had been.[37] Even forty years later the memory of the natural beauty of northern New Hampshire was something these surviving former prisoners of war prized; they spoke of the clear lakes, the tumbling waterfalls, the endless forest, the massive trees, the deep drifts of snow, the steep hillsides ablaze with fall foliage.

Camp Stark itself was less lovely. The Germans were surprised to find that such primitive quarters would be their next abode. Until they arrived at Camp Stark their prisoner-of-war experience in America had placed them in prison compounds attached to American military bases. They had enjoyed accommodations similar to the best the United States provided for its own enlisted men, certainly superior to what they had known as a penal division of the Germany army. Camp Stark was a big step down. The nine narrow wooden buildings that formed the small camp were functional but bleak.[38] As they were assigned barracks and bunks, the Germans began to realize that ordinary living here could be hard. A chill wind whistled by the door. The camp grounds were rough and muddy. The latrine was 200 yards away. A glance across the road revealed that the American army guards occupied quarters no less primitive.

Some of the Germans assumed that before the war Camp Stark must have been a prison work camp for hardened American criminals.[39]

Then the American major spoke. He was an older man. Some of the Germans wondered if he had fought against their country in World War I.[40] Speaking through a U.S. Army interpreter, he said that this was a dangerous place. He called their attention to the fence. The fence surrounding the camp, he said, was not to keep them in as much as it served to protect them from the local population. The people who lived in these mountains, he explained, were French-Canadian. They spoke only French. They all carried rifles. They were half-wild, hostile people. They hated Germans. If any prisoner were to escape into the surrounding forests, he would be shot by one of these gun-toting natives. Or he would be attacked and eaten by the bears that prowled the forest at night. Most of the prisoners of war were more amused than frightened by the major's description of the local population. But there was something about the major which warned them that he was a man to be feared.[41]

Easter Sunday dawned. For many of the Germans it was but one of many holidays in captivity. The political prisoners and the criminals from the 999 who were among the first shipment of prisoners to Stark had spent their share of holidays in German jails or concentration camps. Two Easters ago they had been in Europe. The last Easter passed in North Africa. Now they lived on yet another continent. That afternoon they walked to the fence to watch the cars drive by. In Germany, civilian traffic had all but disappeared. Here in a remote hard-pressed corner of wartime American people still went for Sunday afternoon drives. Some of the Germans felt embarrassed and even angry, being stared at like animals in a cage. Others shook their heads and smiled as some of the passing American girls waved.

5

Strife in a Bitter Place

No one expected anything significant to happen at Camp
Stark. As far as the U.S. Army and the Brown Company were
concerned, Camp Stark existed for a single reason: pulpwood.
Any activity that increased the amount of pulpwood it produced
was good; any activity that decreased it was bad. The army and
the company put the Germans to work immediately. Few of the
Germans at Camp Stark had ever held an axe before, but the
demand to get the project under way encouraged the army to
rush them into the woods with only minimal training in
woodsmanship.

By mid-April 1944, the first trainload of arriving prisoners
of war had been joined by additional men sent up from Fort
Devens. The daily schedule started early, with reveille at 5:30 or
sometimes 5:00 A.M.[1] Fifteen minutes later the Germans lined
up for roll call and to be counted. Following breakfast, they
reported to the main gate to be counted once again as they
boarded the trucks bound for the work sites. The Germans were
counted several times a day, sometimes several times in succes-
sion by guards who seemed to have trouble counting.[2] The ride
to the cutting took them two or three miles down the road or
perhaps ten miles up a neighboring brook valley. Eventually the
German loggers of Camp Stark traveled even to woodlots in
Vermont. Sometimes the cutting area was too rough or steep for
vehicles, and the workers were forced to walk from the trucks.
Climbing up steep, rocky slopes and fording swollen streams
while carrying axes and saws could make the trip to work more
difficult than the job itself. Once at the cutting site, the prisoners

of war operated in groups of thirty to forty men. For security reasons, each garment of their army-issue clothing was marked prominently on the front and back with "PW." Armed guards patrolled the perimeter of the cutting area. The larger group was further divided into work crews, usually of five men. Two men felled and limbed the trees, one man worked with the horse to twitch the trees to the loading area, two men cut the trees to the appropriate lengths.[3] At first the work day lasted nine hours. In warm weather the workers brought their noon meal with them, usually sandwiches. In cold weather trucks delivered a hot meal to the Germans and the guards at noon. At the end of the work day the trucks returned the men to the camp. After being counted again, cleaning up, and eating dinner, the evening was theirs.

Since pulpwood was the reason for everyone's being there, the continuing question was "How much?" Experienced woodsmen normally produce between two and three cords of wood per man per day. The army and the Brown Company assumed that with practice the prisoners of war could be expected to produce one cord per man per day, *"eine Klafter pro Kopf."* At first, however, the quota was established at three-quarters of a cord per man per day. The prisoners of war used only hand saws and axes, although the camp possessed one chain saw—by a curious irony, a heavy, unwieldy, temperamental machine of German manufacture, accompanied by instructions in German encoded for military purposes. It was used only rarely by Brown Company employees for cutting new roads in the woods.[4] In addition to their quota of pulpwood, the German workers needed to cut enough firewood for all cooking and heating in Camp Stark—about seven hundred cords per year. This requirement, opposed by the army and the company, stemmed from a visit in the summer of 1944 of the Truman Committee to prisoner-of-war logging camps in Maine. Truman fumed when he learned that coal was being shipped to wood camps, and he made a snap decision that they should burn nothing except wood. The decision stood, even though it remained more convenient and cheaper to buy coal than to employ prisoners of war to cut firewood.[5] Whether it was pulpwood or firewood, the Germans were forced to cut their daily quota. The quota caused problems from the first day, and helped to make Camp Stark, in the summer of 1944, a bitter place.

Eventually Camp Stark would win acclaim as a place where enemies learned to get along with each other and even to like each other. It did not start out that way. At the beginning there was trouble between the Americans and Germans, trouble among the Germans, and trouble among the Americans. On the American side of the camp the atmosphere was contentious. Sometimes the cause was more or less normal for army life, like resentment over one adept poker player's ability to win much of the payroll. However, some men in the first contingent of guards at Camp Stark came from trouble or failure at a previous assignment, and they fomented a high level of discontent.[6] At times they verbally abused the Germans, and even poked them with a rifle or pricked them with a bayonet. There always was the danger that a frustrated guard might bring the shooting war to the prison camp. This never happened at Camp Stark, where no guard ever fired a shot, but there were enough incidents in prisoner-of-war camps throughout the country to make it a legitimate concern.[7] (The worst incident occurred in Utah when an American soldier on guard duty in a watchtower suddenly sprayed prisoner tents below with machinegun fire, killing nine and wounding twenty.)[8]

Forty years later, as recollection of the Camp Stark story adjusted itself to fit its larger significance, some of the guards would recall incorrectly, as others would maintain, that they had been ordered never to shoot.[9] There were, however, orders prohibiting conversation between the American soldiers and the Germans. The tense atmosphere of the first months of Camp Stark enforced the army's strict nonfraternization policy. The Americans watchfully kept their distance from the Germans, whether manning the machine guns in the four watchtowers at the corners of the stockade or patrolling the perimeter of the work area, carbine in hand.[10] Although the guards never fired these weapons at a prisoner of war at Camp Stark, one German suffered a bullet wound. On the way to the work site one day, a truck became stuck climbing a steep hill. The guard jumped out, intending to push the truck. He threw his rifle back into the cab, and it discharged, sending a bullet through the shoulder of a stunned prisoner of war riding in back. The wound was not serious, but he was taken to the hospital in Berlin to recover. In one of the first gestures of friendship between the Germans and Americans of Stark, several local people stopped by at the hospital to see him.[11]

These overtures of friendship were not common, however, during the first spring and summer. The relations between the Germans and the Americans worsened because of the Germans' inability or unwillingness to meet their wood quota. The Germans complained that woodcutting was unusually difficult and even dangerous work.[12] The quota was too high, they claimed, and too inflexible. It made no allowance for differences in the stand of trees in which the cutting was to be done. Large trees increased the daily production, while small spindly ones added up very slowly.[13] By mid-May a crisis had developed. Major Edgar Schwartz, the camp commander, countered the prisoners' low production by increasing the work day to twelve hours, and raising the daily quota to one and a half cords per man. When the Germans responded by threatening to go on strike, the major summoned them together, and informed them that he was obliged to do his duty. They could appeal to the Swiss legation, but in the meantime they must work. The Germans were shaken by his threat that he had enough gas and other means to turn the camp into a cemetery.[14]

Individual prisoners of war who failed to meet their quota or who mistreated the woodcutting tools were thrown in a special stockade and placed on a diet of bread and water. This punishment exacerbated the ill-feelings not only between the Germans and the major, but also between the guards and the Germans because it required an American guard to stay awake all night guarding the malfeasants.[15] Although the work day was soon cut back again to nine hours, the quota remained, and working conditions worsened with the arrival of that springtime scourge of the north woods, black flies and mosquitoes. The Germans had never encountered such savage insects. The little beasts produced groans of recollection even forty years later. Smoky fires and home-remedy bug dope shared by the civilian foremen proved equally ineffective. Tempers shortened on both sides of the fence, and guard-prisoner relations worsened. Somehow the

Germans had befriended a stray dog, which they trained to snarl at the Americans. At least one civilian foreman began to pack a pistol to protect himself from the apparently vicious animal, prompting one of the American officers to shoot the dog as a quick lesson to the Germans about who was in charge.[16] Ill-will between the Americans and Germans grew, fostered by still further incidents. The prisoners of war, appealing to their Geneva Convention right to be free from public insults, objected to buses of children singing "God Bless America" as they passed the camp. The major, who seemed to vacillate between oppression and concession, agreed, which did not sit well with the local people and prompted an angry inquiry by Senator Styles Bridges.[17]

Meanwhile, the Germans continued to fall short of their quota. Camp Stark in time was to earn several reputations. Its eventual national press and television coverage would make it perhaps the most widely known of America's World War II prisoner-of-war camps. But that would come much later. Its first reputation was not distinguished. Camp Stark was easily the most unproductive pulpwood camp in the Northeast. By the summer of 1944, the same pulpwood shortages that had created it to begin with had given birth to other pulpwood camps—Seboomook, Spencer Lake, and Princeton, all in northern Maine. While Camp Stark struggled to eke out a daily production of .42 cords per man, these other camps came close to their quota of one cord.[18] To some people, the reason for the difference seemed easy to discern. Camp Stark was a camp where anti-Nazis formed the majority, while the others were all Nazi camps. This tended to confirm the prevailing opinion among American officials: anti-Nazis were lazy trouble-makers; Nazis were hard-working and obedient, making life easier for their captors.

Even after forty years, the surviving Americans of Camp Stark would not understand fully the role of politics in the camp and the role of politics in recent German history. Although later the Americans were quick to say, "These Germans here were mostly anti-fascists," at first they paid no heed to the prisoners' politics. All they understood, or sought to understand, was that politics hurt pulpwood production. Yet political issues would give rise to another of Camp Stark's reputations, and political struggles would distinguish the camp.

From the beginning, politics played a central and confused role in the Camp Stark story. It was an anti-Nazi camp because the majority of its prisoner-of-war population were anti-Nazis from the penal (later Afrika) Division 999. In some ways this gave the camp itself a different appearance. In many of the United States' German prisoner-of-war camps, especially Nazi camps, the prisoners donned their German army uniforms on Sundays or even at the end of the work day. Most of the men at Camp Stark rarely wore their German uniforms. The Camp Stark Germans insisted on electing their spokesman rather than allowing rank to determine him.[19] None of this meant, however, that all the Germans at Camp Stark were anti-fascists. Many of the actual criminals in the 999 held Nazi beliefs. Additional shipments of prisoners of war from Fort Devens included Nazis who had been erroneously sent to the large anti-Nazi camp in Massachusetts. So, although Camp Stark maintained an anti-Nazi majority, there were always some ardent Nazis among them, and the anti-Nazis had trouble maintaining a solid front against the Nazis.

In much the same way that the Popular Front, which united socialists and communists in the fight against fascism in Europe in the 1930s, proved fragile, so Camp Stark was plagued by division between its socialists and its democrats. The communists were dedicated, zealous, prone to use force. The more numerous Social Democrats were uncertain of their relationship to the communists and to each other. The anti-fascists in Camp Stark often seemed more united by their fear of fascism than by their actions against it. They all remembered how readily fascism in their homeland had grown from a fringe minority to a totalitarian dictatorship. This memory explained their consternation when a handful of Nazis in the camp attempted to celebrate Hitler's birthday on April 20, 1944.

Moreover, the anti-fascists became concerned not only about the Nazis within the camp, but also about the possibility of the triumph of fascism in America. Anti-fascist prisoners of war were disturbed by American guards' preference for dealing with "obedient" Nazi prisoners of war rather than democratically inclined anti-fascists who discussed and questioned everything. One morning shortly after the camp opened, while snow still clung to the dome-shaped Percy Peaks just to the north of Stark, a group of anti-fascists in the camp expressed dismay at what appeared to be a large swastika tramped in the snow on the nearest mountain peak. They were convinced that the rough swastika, probably formed naturally by ledges appearing through the melting snow, had been carved by American sympathizers with Nazism. The anti-Nazis voiced similar concern to each other about the camp commander's methods of enforcing the quota. The hard work in the woods was made worse by their perception of the major's "fascist" attitude and behavior.[20] The anti-fascists never lost their fear that their battle with fascism might continue on the American continent.

Preoccupation with politics lowered pulpwood production. Many of the anti-Nazi prisoners of war became convinced that they should not be forced to labor for the Americans nor should they suffer the same incarceration as the Nazis. They felt their anti-Nazi credentials entitled them to preferential treatment. They wanted to be welcomed by the Americans as allies in a common struggle. They shared these convictions with each other, their fellow prisoners, and even the American guards and foremen whenever they could. Instead of cutting wood, they spent their time talking, persuading, debating—behavior the Americans interpreted as laziness, trouble-making, political agitation. Eventually, the Camp Stark authorities transferred thirty of their most active anti-Nazis to a newly opened prisoner-of-war base camp in Houlton, Maine.[21] The remaining anti-Nazi prisoners of war maintained their conviction that in the long run their political discussions with Germans and Americans contributed more to the larger Allied war objective than did cutting pulpwood. Perhaps they were right.

By late spring, news from the war brought hope and sorrow. The Normandy invasion signaled the beginning of the end for the Nazi regime. By now all the Camp Stark prisoners of war, whatever their politics, realized that they would go home only after the defeat of Germany. This realization led to emotional dilemmas. They cheered each step that brought closer the end of the war but then experienced waves of guilt and anguish because of hoping for the defeat of their homeland. They knew that defeat would not come easily, and that among the people who would pay the highest price were their own loved ones in Germany. Each week the mail brought notice of wives, children, or parents killed or injured in American and British bombing raids. Personal anxiety about distant family members, fatigue from working long hours in the woods, political differences, cramped quarters, and, on top of everything else, a long heat wave increased tension.

Now, the main problems were not between the Germans and the Americans, but between Germans and Germans. Prison camps, even in the best of times, are not happy places. Camp Stark was becoming an increasingly unhappy place. Confinement itself, with many men living too close together for too long, created problems. When a new group of sixty prisoners of war arived from Fort Devens word quickly spread that they had been shipped to Stark to rid Devens of troublemakers.[22] American civilian foremen arriving at the camp early in the morning noticed prisoners nursing black eyes or swollen jaws.[23] A prisoner of war caught cheating at cards ran to the American guards begging for protection from his fellow Germans until tempers cooled.[24] The squabbles and tension inside the prisoner-of-war compound became more than some men could bear. They ran away.

With the first escapes in the summer of 1944, Camp Stark began to earn a reputation as one of America's least secure prisoner-of-war camps. The American government had worried about escapes from the moment it locked up its first prisoner of war. Visions of escaped Nazi soldiers rampaging across the United States, sabotaging military installations lay behind the War Department's initial refusal early in the war to agree to accept thousands of Germans captured by the British. Once that argument was lost and the prisoners of war began to arrive, the War Department insisted that the prisoner-of-war camps be located in regions of the country where security could be assured. Camp commanders received countless memos and warnings to maintain their vigilance against prisoners determined to escape. Civilian concerns about the dangers of escaping prisoners of war were fueled by alarmist articles in popular magazines like one entitled, "Enemies at Large," by F.B.I. Director J. Edgar Hoover.[25] After several months, the American authorities began to realize that their concerns about mass escapes were largely unfounded. Most of the German prisoners of war demonstrated no desire to flee. For many, especially in the larger camps, which offered a full recreation program to keep the prisoners of war occupied in their free time, life was tolerable. Above all, there seemed to be no place to go. The long train ride to the camps had demonstrated the size of the United States. Fleeing east or west would bring the escapee only to the edge of a large ocean. To the north lay Canada, to the south Mexico, both at war with Germany and pledged to apprehend any escaped prisoner of war.[26] In Europe, escaped American prisoners of war could hope to make their way to neutral Switzerland, Spain, or Sweden, often with the help of resistance organizations in Nazi-occupied Europe. No such sanctuaries awaited escaped German prisoners of war, nor could they rely upon American civilian assistance.

These obstacles to escape deterred most German prisoners of war, but not all. Some German prisoners of war escaped simply because they were expected to. The Geneva Convention stated that prisoners of war were bound by duty to attempt to escape.[27] None did so with the intent to commit sabotage or crimes. A few, usually dedicated Nazis, escaped from American prisoner-of-war camps in order somehow to make their way back to Germany.[28] None succeeded. Most of the escaping prisoners of war were motivated by nothing more than the desire to get away, to be alone, to taste freedom. As time went on and more prisoners of war poured into the United States, the number of escapes increased accordingly. Once the American authorities decided that escaped German prisoners of war posed no threat to public safety, they relaxed their guard. The expansion of the prisoner-of-war labor program took prisoners to lightly guarded work sites in fields and forests. Sometimes they could escape simply by walking away. However, escapes were not without risk, especially in the large base camps. Although guards were ordered to issue a verbal warning and wait until the last second before firing their rifles at an escaping prisoner, fifty-six German prisoners of war were shot to death in a variety of escape attempts in the United States during World War II.[29] The number of escapes nationwide rose from 81 in 1943 to 1,028 in 1944 to about 3 per day in 1945. However, this escape ratio was lower than that of most federal penitentiaries.[30]

Some of the escapes from German prisoner-of-war camps in the United States involved months of planning, forged documents, and reconstructed clothing. Perhaps the most noteworthy was the Christmas Eve 1944 escape of twenty-five, mostly U-boat officers, from the German prisoner-of-war camp at Papago Park, Arizona.[31] Although ingenuity and courage might enable men to escape, they did not always bring a long time in freedom. Most escapees were recaptured within twenty-four hours, and almost all were back behind the fence within three days. They were usually apprehended by civilian authorities. A few remained at large for several weeks, and seventeen escapees succeeded in melting into the American population for years. One made good his escape after learning what not to do from J. Edgar Hoover's famous article warning about escaped prisoners of war.[32] Eventually each was apprehended or turned himself in, the last fugitive German prisoner of war surrendering only in 1985.[33]

The first escape from Camp Stark was noticed when one man was missing from the count at the end of a work day. Immediately an alarm was broadcast. Local and state police were notified, the F.B.I. was informed, and the army guards fanned into the woods in pursuit of the fugitive. Word spread quickly throughout the village that one of the Germans had escaped. Mothers pulled their children inside their houses to safety. One elderly gentleman showed up at the camp dressed in his Spanish-American War uniform, complete with leggings and rifle. He saluted the commander, announced that he had returned to active duty, and headed for the woods.[34] It was all over by evening. A local civilian had spotted the escaped prisoner of war and called the police. He was back in Camp Stark by 9 P.M.[35] But he was the first of many.

Escapes became easy and common at Camp Stark in the summer of 1944. The small branch camp suffered—or boasted—probably the highest escape rate of any U.S. prisoner-of-war camp. At one time or another over 10 percent of Camp

Stark's prisoner population was "on the lam." In one busy month, 19 Germans took to the woods. Escape from the stockade itself was almost impossible. Only one German managed an unauthorized exit from within the camp proper, helped by a fast tongue and a slow-witted guard. He presented himself at the main gate and simply talked his way out, saying something about needing to fetch ice for the prisoner-of-war canteen. After a night spent in the woods, he was apprehended next morning by two soldiers as he walked along the road to Berlin. He and the inattentive guard received their respective punishments.[36]

The Geneva Convention stipulated that prisoners of war were subject to the regulations of the captor army, and recommended a series of punishments including verbal reprimand, loss of pay and privileges, extra labor, dietary restriction for up to fourteen days, special confinement for up to thirty days.[37] Camp Stark escapees and other disciplined prisoners of war were usually confined to a special 4-cell stockade and placed on a diet of bread and water for between three and fourteen days. Often their heads were shaved, ostensibly as a sanitation measure, but also to brand and stigmatize them.[38]

Although escape from Camp Stark itself was almost impossible to accomplish, escape from the work site in the woods was almost impossible to prevent. A prisoner of war merely had to hide under a brush pile at the end of the day, stay there until the others had left, and then he was free to roam. Apart from the increasing personal tensions among prisoners, several factors prompted the rash of escapes in the first summer of Camp Stark. The unusually hot weather invited nights under the open sky. A bountiful crop of wild berries assured escapees of at least some nourishment. None of the escaping prisoners sought to return to Germany.[39] Most made no attempt to travel far. They just wanted some time to be free.

When prisoners of war escaped, press notices often accompanied by "mug shots" appeared in local and sometimes in Boston papers. The army guards were posted in the woods wherever two trails crossed. If they saw the escapee they were ordered to shout "Halt!" If that failed to stop him, they were to shoot a warning shot, and only after that shoot to wound.[40] But none of the Camp Stark guards who whiled away hours at lonely trail junctions ever spotted an escaped prisoner of war.[41] Most of the escaped prisoners of war attempted to surrender, when the time came, to civilians. They feared the wrath of American servicemen angry about having to spend time searching the woods, often at the expense of an evening pass to Berlin. One time two Germans recaptured along Philips Brook were forced to jog over ten miles back to the camp as a guard sat on the front of a jeep, jabbing them with his bayonet.[42] Eventually, as escape and recapture became almost routine, people calmed down. Sometimes no search was mounted. The army would telephone the F.B.I., whose agents drove to the camp and waited until someone called in, saying he had seen or even apprehended the escaped German.[43] The press began to assume a slightly bemused attitude. After three escaped prisoners of war had been picked up more than twenty miles from the camp, an article in the *Berlin Reporter* noted that "judging from the amount of ground covered, the prisoners must have been formerly in Rommel's army and were fleet of foot in retreat," and went on to chasten the camp command for "these all too frequent leaves of absence: With six such escapes in a little over a week, surely the authorities themselves should be on the alert to put an end to the stop-and-scoot practices of the Germans at Stark."[44]

Oddly enough, these escapes paved the way for the future accord betwen the Stark villagers and the Germans. Once people realized that the escaped prisoners of war posed no serious threat, they began to chuckle at some of the misguided, frenzied efforts of the authorities and to feel a little sympathy for the Germans who sought the freedom of the countryside. Escapes also made life in Stark more exciting. False leads phoned in by local residents eager to help proved a problem for police and innocent civilians. Twice police hurried to the scene only to find a surprised fisherman. Three times in one day Berlin police investigated the same solitary man who simply enjoyed wandering about by himself.[45] One local woman saw two escaped prisoners of war across her field, playing with some horses. She waited a while, then called the police after they had moved along. One escaped German made his way up Mill Brook, stopping at "Mr. Mayhew's camp." Mr. Mayhew asked him if he escaped from the prison camp. The German said he had, that he was tired of always being told what to do there. While Mr. Mayhew continued the conversation, his son snuck out and telephoned the authorities. When they finally arrived, the German was still talking with his new American friend. Mr. Mayhew, the captors said, was a good talker.[46]

Escapes continued all summer and into the early fall. Some went awry in less than a day, while others lasted more than a week. Two escaped Germans turned themselves in at the main gate after becoming sick on more than two days' diet of berries, probably some of the wrong sort. One prisoner of war who escaped while cutting in the forest thought he had won his way to freedom when his travels brought him to a boxcar on a railroad siding. He climbed aboard, hoping to be far from Camp Stark as soon as the car was moved, not knowing that it was broken down and destined to be parked there all winter. He ended up back at the camp in a few days.[47] Another escapee headed east through the forest, climbed up Milan Hill, and took refuge in the fire tower at the top. To ward off the evening chill, he made a fire in the stove. Valley dwellers, knowing the tower was closed, saw the smoke and called the authorities.[48] Two prisoners of war, Gerhard Prager and Johann Sarstedt escaped twice in one week, the second time getting as far as Gilead, Maine before their recapture.[49] Twice in late August civilian campers near South Pond, anxious to do their patriotic duty as well as to collect the $15 bounty offered for each returned prisoner of war, corralled missing Germans.[50] A two-day manhunt for three escaped prisoners of war ended easily when they were picked up in downtown Lancaster, N.H., twenty miles away. They had used razor blades to scratch the "PW" off their army shirts and trousers. They spent their afternoon of freedom casually sauntering along the main street, window shopping, until the slanting rays of the declining sun brought out the faint outline of the letters etched on their clothes, ending their brief taste of civilian life.[51] Bruno Leipner and Johann Hoffman managed to avoid recapture for nearly two weeks. They slipped into the fog at the end of a day of woodcutting near West Milan and remained in the forest for four days, then began walking the roads at night, heading southwest, passing through Lancaster and Whitefield. They became separated, and each continued on his way. The weary Hoffman accepted a ride from a passing motorist. His benefactor proved to be the police chief in Lisbon, N.H. who drove him straight to jail, and called the F.B.I. Leipner was captured by the Woodsville police chief three days later.[52] Another law officer proved less diligent. A deputy sheriff picked up a hitch-hiking escaped German, and drove him all the way to the Canadian border, believing the thick-accented man's story that he was a Dutch sailor returning to his ship in Montreal. When he was detained by Canadian border authorities he confessed, saying he was on his way to see his uncle who was a German prisoner of war in Canada. He was sent back to Stark.[53]

The cooler nights of the approaching autumn slowed the escape rate, although Siegfried Tatzko, "the gypsy," as he was scornfully called, made one more attempt. Tatzko, an acrobat and a loner, was shunned by his fellow prisoners of war, who said he was mentally unstable. They wanted nothing to do with him, and he felt the same way about them. So the Americans allowed him to live by himself, first in a tent, and then in the punishment stockade on the American side of the road. Tatzko became responsible for tending the cooking and heating fires in the American compound. But these privileges were not enough to dampen his desire to escape. His first attempt had resulted in his easy apprehension as he made his way along the road. The second, on October 2, took him to the side of Dummer Hill, where he dug a little cave, squirreled away some apples, turnips, and cattle mash stolen from nearby farms, and prepared to burrow in for the winter. Two local hunters stumbled upon Tatzko and his dugout. They quickly convinced him that he could never survive the New Hampshire winter in his little earthen home and escorted him back to the warmth of Camp Stark.[54]

Every prisoner-of-war story should have a tunnel. Camp Stark had its tunnel in November 1944. Carl Schmurr and Fritz Pusch slept in the upper and lower bunks in the corner of barracks number one, nearest the watchtower by the road. Schmurr had made trouble for the camp authorities since he arrived. He claimed to be a second officer in the German Merchant Marine, and therefore maintained that he should be in an officer prisoner-of-war camp, not an enlisted man's labor camp. He decided to escape to make his way to Washington to plead his case. He asked Pusch if he wanted to help dig. Pusch later said that he wanted to get away from the communists in Camp Stark, so he agreed to help. Apparently, although other men in the barracks knew about the tunnel, only Pusch and Schmurr did the digging. Pusch worked in the camp carpentry shop and had access to tools. The two men sawed a trap door in the floor under their bunks and then dug a large pit where they stored their supplies. The dirt was scattered under the raised barracks floor. Digging on Sundays and at night, they produced a remarkable tunnel over 30 feet long, 2 feet high, and 18 inches wide. It was shored with boards picked up around the camp. Pilfered wire brought electric light from a ceiling socket. To supply themselves on their escape they gathered a variety of clothes and a cache of food including 2 loaves of pumpernickel bread, 2 pounds of cookies, 27 bags of peanuts, and 2 pounds of ham. The American guards discovered the tunnel, not through their own diligence but through a German informer. At the time the tunnel was revealed, Schmurr and Pusch were less than ten feet from the drainage ditch under the guard tower, which was the target of their tunnel. Had they reached it, escape from the camp without being seen would have been easy. Senior officers at the base camp at Fort Devens reprimanded the Camp Stark personnel for their failure to locate and report the tunnel sooner. The two German diggers were sent to other camps for appropriate punishment. The tunnel was filled in and tamped down.[55]

Camp Stark's most famous escape was that of Franz Bacher. A short, ruddy, 27-year-old Austrian from Vienna, Bacher was an accomplished artist, and spoke English, Italian, French, and German fluently. An amiable man, he detested military life. He used his art to win friends. During short breaks in the woods, he would sit on a stump producing an admirable drawing, which he then gave to the civilian foreman. Other drawings and oil paintings went to the first sergeant and other guards. Bacher paintings of mosques in North Africa (where he was captured with others of the 999) and of mountains in New Hampshire decorated the walls of homes in Stark, Berlin, and Milan for years following the war. Bacher also used his artistic talent to make money as well as friends. Guards received paintings of their wives or girlfriends; Bacher obtained, against strict regulations, the American currency he would need for his escape. After somehow acquiring a civilian jacket, he painted "PW" on the back in watercolor. On August 1, he wore the jacket to work, hid in the brush, washed off the incriminating letters in a stream, and was gone.

When Bacher failed to show up to be counted at the end of the day, the guards, following usual procedures, checked his bunk and belongings for clues. On his bed they found a note:

> I am going to escape today. The reason I am doing this is I live for my art. If I continue to cut wood, my hands will become so mutilated that I will be unable to paint. If I can't paint, I can do nothing.[56]

Meanwhile Bacher was hiking more than twenty miles across the Kilkenny Wilderness until he emerged on U.S. Route 2 in Jefferson, N.H. There, in front of one of the large hotels, he hopped on a bus and rode south, eventually reaching New York City. He went right to work, supporting himself by selling pictures he painted in Central Park. After sleeping in the park for nearly a month, Bacher rented a room on St. Mark's Place. He seemed to have successfully melted into American society.

Meanwhile, back at Camp Stark, rumors flew about the fate of Franz Bacher, the camp's only prisoner of war to elude capture for more than a month. First it was said that he had been shot, with three bullets in the back, at the Canadian border. Then the rumor spread that he had made it safely to Canada. Still another rumor alleged he had been seen in New York City. The prisoner of war who had agreed to inform Bacher's parents should an accident befall him wondered what to do.

One Sunday morning in early October 1944, Bacher was walking through Penn Station, one of the thousands of wartime travelers who jammed that station every Sunday. With a mixture of anguished disbelief and strange pleasure, he bumped into someone he knew: the U.S. Army interpreter from Camp Stark, who happened to be in New York City on a 3-day leave. Both men were astounded by the chance encounter more than four hundred miles from Camp Stark. The irony, however, was doubled. Both men were from Vienna. Their homes in Austria had been only a few blocks apart.

Sergeant Ted Tausig, the American interpreter at Camp Stark, had known several near-misses. An Austrian Jew, he had barely escaped the Nazis in his own country. When he and other family members were having their emigration requests processed in a Nazi office, most of his family were sent to the line on the left. He was motioned to the right. Those in the line on the right made their way to London. Those on the left ended their lives in Dachau. Once in England, Tausig applied for transit to the United States. Just as war was about to break out, his papers were approved suddenly. Tausig rushed to leave, but missed his ship to America. The ship, the *Athenia,* never made it. It was sunk by a U-boat on the first day of the war. When he finally arrived in New York, Tausig worked his trade, embroidering handbags, until called by the U.S. Army. A training injury kept him from overseas duty; his native German language sent him to a German prisoner-of-war camp. In Stark, Tausig and Bacher had become friends. They shared a home city, a cultural heritage, similar leftist political views, and aesthetic values. There in Penn Station the two men spoke briefly, on friendly terms, and went their separate ways.

The complete story of what happened next may never be known. Tausig, the new immigrant to the United States, wanted to do the right thing for his new country and the right thing for his fellow Austrian. Several days later, Bacher was arrested by F.B.I. agents and then sent to Fort Devens. He was apprehended at an art supply store in Union Square. Apparently he tipped his hand when he asked for paint known only to German artists. At least, that was one of the official versions. Another credited the F.B.I. for circulating his photograph to art supply stores in New York City.[57] After the war Bacher met a friend from Camp Stark as they were being processed through Fort Eustis, Virginia, before their repatriation. Bacher said he had talked with Tausig, but thought that Tausig had not turned him in.[58] Tausig said that as an American soldier, not knowing what Bacher planned to do, he had no choice except to call the authorities.[59] But he may have delayed while he thought it over.

Something had to change at Camp Stark. The low pulpwood

production, the strife inside the camp, the high escape rate, all pointed to changing the camp commander. Prisoner-of-war camp commanders probably never elicit unanimous opinions on their performance. Major Edgar Schwartz, an elderly World War I veteran of the 389th field artillery, had those who admired him for his intellect and his habit of choosing Shakespeare as his bedside reading.[60] But many others judged him ill-suited for commanding Camp Stark. He was perceived both by prisoners of war and guards as disliking the Germans intensely. Some of the guards wondered if the major hoped for a shooting incident to set an example for the prisoners. The anti-fascist Germans compared his attitudes and actions to those of Hitler and Mussolini.[61] When the complaints about Schwartz's performance appeared in correspondence between the First Service Command Headquarters in Boston and the Brown Company, his days at Stark were numbered. On September 24, 1944 Schwartz was relieved by a 31-year-old captain, Alexandium Kobus.[62] The new camp commander came from the pulpwood prisoner-of-war camp in Princeton, Maine, where he had won the reputation of bringing order out of chaos.

Captain Kobus turned first to the problem of pulpwood production. After meeting with the Brown Company officials and foremen, American military personnel, and the German prisoners of war, he determined that the low pulpwood production, now sunk to one quarter cord per man per day, was due to problems in supervision, instruction, personnel, diet, and camp procedures. Kobus inaugurated a 2-week training period in wood cutting. He insisted that the foremen provide closer supervision in the woods, making sure each prisoner of war was part of a 5-man work crew. Each crew had a quota, which at first amounted to $\frac{1}{2}$ cord per man per day, later raised to $\frac{3}{4}$ cord, then to 1 cord. All prisoners were given physical examinations, with those found unfit for the work exchanged for others from Fort Devens. Prisoners were allowed to return to camp only for sickness or injury. Complaints to the camp commander could be made only at the close of the work day. (Schwartz had allowed the prisoners to leave the work site any time to make a complaint.)

The atmosphere in the camp seemed to settle down, responding perhaps to a new sense of order. But to some prisoners of war the quota still seemed too high. When a group of thirty prisoners failed to meet their quota, Kobus concluded that it was an attempt to reduce the quota to three-quarters of a cord. He placed the recalcitrant workers in newly erected squad tents outside the camp, but surrounded by barbed wire. There they were required to cut firewood in the evenings until dark. Their daily food ration was reduced to match their quota reduction. If they produced three-quarters of their quota, they received three-quarters of their food. Within two weeks they had returned to a full cord per day, a full daily ration, and their regular barracks.[63] Ultimately, the practice of requiring the prisoners of war to work overtime to reach their quota and reducing their ration accordingly if the problem persisted served to assure full production.

Next, Captain Kobus changed many of the guards. Except for those with military police training, he replaced most of the guards with combat veterans. The unsuitable guards, he discovered, were in some ways cowed by the Germans and in other ways abusive toward them. Combat veterans tended to be more professional, more detached. There was the danger that one might bring home with him battle-bred hatred of the Germans. But in general combat veterans seemed to be fairer to the Germans than were troops who had not served overseas.[64] Relations between the guards and the prisoners of war did not improve overnight. The continual rotation and changes within American military personnel at Camp Stark brought new problems from time to time. Occasional incidents of guards' abusing prisoners of war persisted. Usually it was verbal abuse, and often it was just showing off. But there were one or two times when a guard struck a prisoner of war with his rifle butt. As soon as cases of verbal or physical abuse were reported to the captain, the offending guard was shipped out.[65] One visit of the International Red Cross gave Camp Stark generally high marks, although the IRC representative objected strenuously on behalf of prisoners who complained that once in a while orders had been enforced by a bayonet nip in the rear. Kobus responded to the inspectors by saying that the Germans at Stark were treated much better than American prisoners in Germany, but the practice would cease.[66]

Kobus also tried to solve a problem with the camp doctors. Camp Stark had had both good and bad experiences with physicians. Two doctors allowed their ethnic heritage to influence the practice of their profession and refused to care adequately for Germans. Both were reassigned. Two others simply hated Camp Stark; one, a gynecologist, understandably felt particularly misplaced.[67] Inadequate or resentful American medical personnel prompted the other Americans to go to the German prisoner-of-war medic, Johann Jarclovski, with their ailments. Years later, some would continue to name him as the best doctor they had ever known. Finally, in Lieutenant Elliot Foster the camp received competent care from its assigned physician.[68]

Captain Kobus made sweeping changes in the American personnel at Camp Stark, but the most important member of his staff had been at Stark from the beginning. Sergeant Tausig, the Viennese-born American interpreter, was placed by Kobus in a position where he could fully utilize his language, communication, and interpersonal skills. As life in Camp Stark began to go more smoothly, much of the credit went to Tausig. Kobus realized that many times Tausig, on his own initiative, convinced the Germans that cooperation with the Americans was to their advantage.[69]

Kobus also moved to end escapes. His allies in this were the onset of colder weather and the coming of order to the work sites. Each guard was responsible for watching two work crews, a ratio of ten prisoners to one guard. But the key to cutting down on escapes was not only more vigilant guards. Kobus had learned that if a German prisoner of war gave his pledge that he would not escape, the Americans could trust his word. The prisoner of war had the right to withdraw his pledge later. Almost all of the prisoners gave this pledge, and only a few later rescinded it.[70] This confidence in the German pledge allowed Kobus to cut back on guards, while giving the entrusted Germans a greater sense of responsibility and freedom. When the United States began its prisoner-of-war program, the War Department planned a prisoner-to-guard ratio of three to one. That proved too rich, and by 1945 the national ratio was nine to one. But at Camp Stark, the pledge not to escape in time allowed a ratio as high as twenty to one.[71]

Finally, Kobus turned to the physical facilities. The former Civilian Conservation Corps camp had fallen into disrepair, and the new barracks for American personnel had been slapped together with many structural flaws. Roofs and windows leaked, fixtures were broken, and most annoying of all, mud was everywhere. The captain put to use the tradesmen among the prisoners of war to dig drainage ditches and repair the buildings. In a few weeks, daily living showed marked improvement. It no longer snowed or rained inside the buildings, and the men could get back and forth to the latrines or showers without wallowing in the mire.[72] Poor sanitation practices under the previous administration had led to an invasion of rats. When poison and traps failed to make a dent in the problem, some of the guards picked up stray cats in Berlin. The rats disappeared.[73]

As far as the officers of the First Service Command Headquarters in Boston were concerned, Camp Stark under Captain Kobus had shaped up. Pulpwood production reached the expected quota, escapes nearly ended, problems seemed to cease. First Service Command General Sherman Miles made regular visits to Camp Stark, walked in the woods with Kobus, and seemed pleased with how smoothly things were going.[74] The Germans were not entirely sure.

During World War I a well-known German saying summed up life in a prisoner-of-war camp: *"Alles hängt vom Kommandanten ab"* ("everything depends on the commander"). The same was true during World War II. In spite of common adherence to the stipulations of the Geneva Convention, life in one prisoner-of-war camp could differ sharply from life in another just a few miles away.[75] It all depended on the camp commander. Camp Stark under Captain Kobus differed from Camp Stark under Major Schwartz. Kobus' primary objective, to which everything else remained subordinate, was to meet the pulpwood production quota. When the prisoners of war failed to produce, he was tough on them. When an American guard interfered with a German's emotional or physical ability to work, he disciplined the guard and removed him. When he discovered that

The abandoned Civilian Conservation Corps camp at Stark, New Hampshire, in the summer of 1943.

The road, barbed-wire fence, barracks, and guard tower are all visible in this view of Camp Stark, after its conversion to a prisoner-of-war camp in 1944.

Camp Stark commander, Capt. Alexandium Kobus, and camp physician, Lt. Elliot Foster.

Prisoner-of-war woodsman receives instructions from
the Brown Company foreman, B. House.

Prisoner-of-war work crew with their American
foreman (front row, second from right).

Entrance to escape tunnel, November 1944.

Escape tunnel after it was discovered by American authorities.

German prisoners of war pose by Sgt. Frank Chappell's jeep.

U.S. Army guard Warren
Hoyt relaxes in front of
axe-toting German prisoner
of war.

German prisoners, in the rear, and American guards
pose with camp pets, including the bear cub.

(on facing page) The parade emerges from the covered bridge at the
start of German-American Friendship Day in Stark.

Forty years after the closing of the prisoner-of-war camp, Stark Town Hall is dressed up for the big day.

Gerhard Clauss toasts his American hosts at the celebration dinner.

Former prisoners-of-war Klaus Wiemann, Hermann Uelsmann, Gerhard Clauss, and Albert Petermann are reunited at Camp Stark, along with their former Brown Company foreman Linwood Gadwah (third from right) and U.S. Army guard Warren Hoyt (second from left).

Brown Company employees were inaccurately counting the cords, not giving the Germans their due, he assigned an American soldier to monitor the count. Kobus thought that his main task as commanding officer, aside from producing pulpwood, was to be fair. With this in mind, he kept his distance from his subordinates and from the prisoners of war. He assumed that the Germans were most likely to obey and respect authority that was stern, remote, above them. Generally, the only prisoner with whom he spoke was young Gerhard Clauss, whose fluent command of English earned him the position of clerk in charge of tallying and reporting the daily pulpwood production. There were some Americans and some Germans who considered the captain too harsh. Some took the brunt of his quick temper. A few wondered if his temper and his Polish heritage occasionally clouded his judgment in dealing with the Germans. But most, on both sides of the fence, agreed that the captain usually achieved his goals of orderly production and fairness.[76]

Yet the camp commander, as well as most of the other American officers, missed much of what happened at Camp Stark. In the autumn of 1944 the prisoner-of-war population in the camp changed significantly. A different kind of prisoner of war began to arrive in a series of shipments from Fort Devens between September and November. The social and political dynamics among the Germans altered and intensified. And the social dynamics between the Germans and the Americans of Stark began to change and intensify also.

The new prisoners had been captured in Normandy shortly after the June 6 Allied invasion. They had been sent first across the English Channel to Great Britain where they were held in large transit camps, often cringing in fear during German V-1 attacks on London. Within several weeks, they were on ships bound for Boston. From there they went to nearby Fort Devens, and then to Camp Stark. Some replaced those original Camp Stark prisoners of war who were deemed physically unfit for work in the woods, while the others brought the camp to its maximum size of about 250 German prisoners of war. The new arrivals differed in age and politics from the 999 veterans who had lived in Camp Stark since it opened. The youth of the Normandy captives testified to the growing shortage of soldiers in

the Third Reich. Most were 18-year olds, while some were
barely seventeen. Their arrival testified to the inevitability of
Germany's defeat and destruction. They had seen and spoken to
other prisoners of the size of the Allied armies that had invaded
Festung Europa. Even more impressively, they had seen the massive supplies of war material in England, waiting to be hurled
against the Germans. Many of them also had seen at first hand
the death and destruction suffered increasingly by German
civilians and cities. The news they brought to Camp Stark from
Europe was sobering and painful.

The two groups of prisoners of war at Camp Stark—*Afrikage-
fangenen* and *Westfrontgefangenen*—were the same that filled other
prisoner-of-war camps throughout the United States.[77] But at
Stark there was an important difference. In most camps the
original *Afrika Korps* captives clung to their military discipline
and to their faith in National Socialism and Hitler. The recent
Normandy captives were more heterogeneous. Some of the
young ones, raised under the Third Reich, remained obdurate
Nazis. An increasingly large segment, however, drafted into
the army as Nazi fortunes declined, was marked by defeatism.
They expressed civilian concerns and assumed an apolitical
posture.[78] This mixed lot of Normandy captives at Camp Stark
encountered the 999 men, *Afrika Korps* captives, who, far from
being hard-core Nazis were hard-core anti-Nazis. The certain
defeat of Nazism now apparent combined with the arrival of the
young men from Europe to stimulate intense renewed political
activity at Camp Stark, which was to earn it yet another reputation as a place of bitter political struggle.

Politics now became the primary pastime in Camp Stark.
The left-wingers who comprised most of the 999 contingent
enjoyed in this remote American prisoner-of-war camp more
political freedom and more political discussion than most of
them had ever known. From the day they arrived in the camp,
the communists and the social democrats argued with each
other and sometimes came to blows. One time a group of communists beat up a political opponent and then informed an
inquiring American guard that the bruised man had fallen from
his bunk.[79] It is—and was—difficult to determine with any
exactitude the political composition of the Camp Stark Ger-

mans. Even after the arrival of the younger prisoners of war, the men of the 999 maintained their majority in the camp, numbering between one-half and two-thirds of the total German population. There were some Nazis in the camp, divided between the criminals from the 999 and the younger group captured in Normandy, who for the first time found themselves a threatened minority in a crowd of Germans. There were several occasions when a group of leftists gleefully beat up a Nazi, enjoying the novel feeling of being on the giving rather than receiving end of political violence. The communists became the most zealous political activists in the camp, and therefore appeared the most numerous; some American military personnel assumed that any anti-Nazi German must be a communist.[80] The report of a visiting and perhaps naively misinformed American major labeled most of the men in Camp Stark as communists. This was not accurate, but the judgment that Camp Stark held a larger percentage of communists than any other prisoner-of-war camp in the United States was probably on the mark.[81]

For a while the communists set the strident tone of Camp Stark. Although recollection in tranquility forty years on was to soften the divisive aspects of Camp Stark and stress the cohesive, it remains true that the communists caused frequent turmoil in the camp. Many of the other prisoners disliked the communists, referring to them as riffraff or objecting to their belligerence. The communists pounced on newly arrived captives, determined to indoctrinate them in their view of the future. Their dialectical debating skills were sharply honed, and their continual proselytizing among the less intense socialists and nonpolitical younger men created constant tension, heated arguments, and frequent fist-fights.[82]

Many of the Germans wearied of the constant political turmoil. Going to work in the woods became the most restful part of the day. Evenings in the German barracks were a time of trial and avoiding confrontation. Not all prisoners of war participated in camp politics. Some barracks were more highly politicized than others. Some men, after initial political skirmishes, simply kept their own counsel on volatile issues.

The political activity at Camp Stark fostered an air of intrigue and mystery. Rumors persisted that somehow there was a

secret connection between the communists in the camp and
Russian diplomats in Washington. The communists seemed to
learn details of postwar political settlements earlier than the
general public.[83] Even among the Americans there were whis-
pers that the American army interpreter reported to intelligence
authorities outside the camp chain of command.[84] People became suspicious and edgy.

In some ways, Camp Stark proved to be a prophetic micro-
cosm of postwar German politics. The Nazis at Camp Stark
learned to keep silent and politically withdrawn. At long last,
they were the ones sought out and punished. The tide of battle
and history had run against them. But they were still there.
They did not disappear, even though they saw little future for
themselves. The anti-fascists were torn between desires never to
remember the Nazis and never to forget them. The communists
were able to enjoy the reputation conferred by their long-term
opposition to fascism. Those who had fought as volunteer soldiers on the Republican side during the Spanish Civil War
could boast that they had risked their lives in the crusade against
fascism while others merely watched. Their association with the
Soviet Union came at the zenith of Allied unity when many people viewed the Red Army as liberators. But these attributes
paled in the face of their argumentative arrogance, strong-arm
tactics, conspiratorial overtones, and personal abrasiveness. At
Camp Stark, communist influence peaked, then ebbed.

The moderate democrats more quietly and more slowly
began to grasp the vision of a democratic, irenic postwar Germany. Camp Stark democrats began to feel part of a wider and
stronger political tradition. They began to see common interests and values linking German and American democracy. German-American publications, produced with American assistance by German prisoners of war at Fort Devens, portrayed the
999 not as the vanguard of Marxism but in the German democratic tradition of 1848 and 1918.[85] Perhaps most important
politically, politics became less important. Twentieth-century
Germans had had enough of politics. The nonpolitical German
prisoners of war began to relax into private interests and to
envision a postwar world in which private lives might become
more important than public concerns. They glimpsed a society

in which politics stayed in its place, and ordinary people did ordinary things.

The camp commander and all but a few of the American officers and guards at Camp Stark knew nothing about all the intense political activity that had been occupying the Germans. They remained oblivious to the issues that concerned the Germans most. But the American presence maintained order and kept things from getting out of hand. In both Camp Stark as later in the American zone of what would become West Germany, the politically naive American military presence contributed to the decline of political extremism and encouraged the growth of moderate democracy and ordinary living.

If the American soldiers at Camp Stark remained out of touch with what was going on there, the civilian population was even more in the dark. Articles appeared regularly in the national and local press recounting the arrival, dispersal, work, "coddling," escapes, and,—finally—departure of the German prisoners of war. Periodicals providing lengthy discussion of their activities ranged from newspapers like the *New York Times* and the *Chicago Tribune* to popular magazines like *Newsweek* and *Colliers* to such specialized publications as the *American Journal of Nursing*. The transportation of nearly 400 thousand Germans to five hundred camps took the prisoner-of-war trains through many communities. The prisoners stepped off the trains to live in confinement near many American towns. Thousands of Americans saw or dealt with them. Yet forty years after the war, many well-informed Americans had no idea that there once had been several hundred thousand German prisoners of war in their country, let alone what political battles had raged among them within the walls of their compounds.

Newspapers in nearby Berlin and Littleton kept their readers informed about the opening of Camp Stark, its contribution to the pulpwood industry, and—with large headlines—escapes from it. The widely read *Manchester Union* carried at least two long feature articles on the camp, including several photographs. The *Boston Post,* widely read in New Hampshire, offered similar coverage. The largest spread on Camp Stark in the *Manchester Union* claimed the center of the front page with a photograph to the right. But the article ran on June 9, 1944, just three days after the D-Day invasion of France. Other news doubtless seemed more important.

Not much seemed significant in Stark as fall gave way to winter in the last months of 1944. The discovery of the tunnel closed the escape season. The camp was in better shape, prepared for the snow and cold. The Germans were learning to be better woodcutters, though not necessarily more willing. The quota still seemed too high to them. At year's end, the quota and the winter cold combined to bring the Americans and the Germans into their sharpest confrontation at Camp Stark: the strike.

The war years saw sad holidays all around the world. Too many homes had too many empty chairs. At Camp Stark, Christmas 1944 was bleak and lonely on both sides of the road. Some of the civilian foremen had said "Merry Christmas" as they had gone home the day before, their eyes showing that they meant it. A few of the prisoners slipped them little home-made trinkets for their children. Some of the Germans had not seen their own children for years. Some had children they had never seen. A few men put up a little Christmas tree in their barracks. In the village, larger Christmas trees lit living rooms—a holiday custom Americans owed to Germans. Inside the stockade there were a few Christmas letters and fewer packages from the war-ravaged homeland. It was a sad Christmas.[86]

Outside a blizzard howled. Arctic winds roared down from Canada. Snow drifted around the barracks and piled up deep in the woods. The next day the temperature dipped colder than $-10°$. The Germans struggled to the work site, wallowing in deep snow. They were afraid that the deep snow might keep them from moving quickly from the path of a falling tree. It was so cold that the axe froze to the tree. Even gloved hands became frozen. That day the prisoners of war failed to come close to the quota. That evening they decided to go on strike next day. They sought abolition of the quota, to be excused from working in harsh weather, and to have the noon meal back at the camp.[87]

The next morning no one reported for roll call. Earlier, the camp commander had prepared to confront a possible strike with dietary restriction, by never delivering more than one day's food ration to the German cooks inside the prisoner-of-war compound. This practice allowed him to place the Germans on a bread-and-water diet immediately. He also closed their canteen. He then ordered the American guards to enter the German barracks to confiscate any food and cigarettes they found there. A quick search netted a large haul: four or five blankets filled with cookies, candy, and cigarettes. The Germans were especially perturbed to lose their supplies since they had paid for them in canteen scrip. A few were able to hide items behind loose boards in the wall. The guards divided up the loot. The strike continued.

Although political concerns prevailed in Camp Stark, the strike had few political overtones. Some of the guards thought it might be connected with the Battle of the Bulge, during which it was called.[88] Some of the vocal anti-Nazis repeated their claim that they should not be required to do any labor.[89] But these were not the issues. The focus remained on the quota and the weather. Each day the prisoners were polled to determine whether they wanted to work or not: *"Arbeiten, oder nicht arbeiten?"* Until the third or perhaps fourth day all replied, *"Nicht arbeiten!"* Eventually, however, the bread-and-water diet took its toll. On the fourth day only fifty refused to work, while two hundred said they would return to the woods. The next day only five said *"Nicht arbeiten!"* The strike ended. The men went back to work. The full food ration was restored. A few of the strike leaders were shipped to another camp.[90]

The exact terms of the settlement remain vague. The quota of one cord was maintained, but if the prisoners of war failed to meet the quota because of bad weather, they would not be punished and could make it up on a subsequent day, using Sundays if necessary. Work was suspended on extremely cold days.

The strike tended to clear the air. Some hard feelings would linger for a while, a long while: forty years later former American guards would joke about confiscating the snacks, but the Germans who recalled Camp Stark did not joke about the strike. They remembered the harsh weather, the bread and water, the hard work, the hard feelings. But in January 1945, the New Year that had begun with the prisoners on strike seemed to hold greater promise. Each side had made its point. More important, each side had seen the other's point. It was a step toward understanding and even respect and friendship.

6

From Barriers to Bonds

It was getting cold at the end of the afternoon. The young German prisoner of war still had some wood to cut in order to meet his quota. He worked a long two-man saw by himself; his partner had been taken away to work on another task. With only one man working it, the long saw bent and buckled. The harder he pushed, the more it buckled. Donald Beattie, the American soldier guarding the area, was getting cold. Beattie came from northern Vermont, just across the Connecticut River from Stark. He knew the climate and the woods. He knew how long he and the prisoner of war would be there at the rate the wood was being cut. He looked at the struggling German and his wobbling saw, and suddenly could stand the sight no longer. He put down his rifle, walked over, and grabbed the other end of the saw. In no time at all the two men zipped through the logs.

"After all," he said later, "it was cold and one man oughtn't work a two-man saw."

It was as simple as that. Work needed to be done the right way. Camp Stark began to change from a bitter place to a decent place as the Americans and the Germans began to realize, perhaps unconsciously, that the barriers which initially divided them had become bonds connecting them.

The war and the work did this to them. The war had brought them to this place and divided them clearly into two sides: American and German, captor and captive, victor and vanquished, outside the fence and inside the fence, north side of the road and south side of the road. The war had become the biggest event in the lives of all of them. The global conflict pushed millions of people around. It had pushed these people to Stark. The Americans and the Germans began to realize that it was here, in Stark, that they would stay probably for the duration. The villagers would remain longer, but no one, neither Germans nor Americans, would go home or back to normal living until the war ended. None had chosen to come to Camp Stark, or to have Camp Stark in their village. Someone else decided all this for them. They were little people, *kleine Leute,* caught in forces beyond their control. The apparent capriciousness of a war that so easily tossed about individual lives, regardless of which side they were on, could nourish empathy between victor and victim. At one time or another, as American guards looked at the Germans inside the fenced compound, they thought that the war just as easily could have made them the prisoners. On both sides of the fence, men knew that others spent the war in better places and in worse places. This was their place and their time together. Gradually, the war, bringing them together in worry and grief, became a shared experience rather than a reason for division. They all feared for loved ones, grieved for lost ones, and joined in hope for an end to the war and for peace. At first the war created or broadened existing divisions between Americans and Germans. At Camp Stark these divisions faded as the war gave them a shared place, shared fears, and shared hopes. As the years went by after its end, the camp also gave them shared memories and eventually shared participation in discovering the significance of their time there and of their role in the war. They were at Camp Stark together because the war had divided them. Because they were there, the war brought them together.

The work that war demanded be done at Camp Stark, cutting pulpwood, led to severe friction between Americans and Germans. But in time the work, like the war, began to bring them together more than it kept them apart. Most people at Camp Stark did not like the wood-cutting business. Only the civilian foremen had chosen that work—usually because there was nothing else to do in Stark. The task of getting pulpwood out of the forest was not easy. And the people of Camp Stark certainly differed among themselves about how fast it was to be accomplished. But the work, like the war, began to be viewed as something big, which had brought all these people together against their will. Initially divisive, work became a unifying activity in the life of Camp Stark.

Adverse climate and terrain helped. At first, the divisions between the people seemed clear. The foremen knew how the work was to be done, the soldiers held the authority, the prisoners of war did the work, the villagers looked on from afar. The distinctions blurred when all trudged through the same blizzard, or sweltered in August heat. Trails to the remote cutting areas were equally steep or muddy for Americans and Germans alike. Together they got to know the hard places and the easy places. In the frozen forest, they warmed themselves by the same fire. They all swatted the same mosquitoes and black flies. They all savored the Indian summer. The work, even more than the war, made shared places and times transcend the differences between people.

Shared attitudes toward work do not follow lines of nationality. Some people are workers. If they see work to be done, they do it. They will not sit idle. They must always be making, producing, carrying, re-arranging. Others seem to live to avoid work. If there is a way out of doing something, they will find it. Most people fall somewhere in the middle, sometimes working enthusiastically, sometimes reluctantly.

It was the worker in that American guard that made him put down his rifle, grab the other end of the saw, and get the job finished in good time and shape. The old Coca-Cola trucks bought by the Brown Company broke down repeatedly. The wheels tended to fall off. When that happened the pace of work had to slow. But the German mechanic could not keep himself from fixing the trucks, getting them back on the road as soon as possible.[1] At the end of the day there were those Germans and Americans who took satisfaction in the stacks of wood that indicated a job well done.

Shirking, as well as working, can create a bond. Sometimes the American guards would maintain an understanding silence when the prisoners of war fooled the foremen by moving the markers on the stacked wood, counting the same pile more than once. Civilian foremen would recall with a smile how slowly some of the Germans worked, about as slowly as Americans if the situation had been reversed. Sometimes the Germans commiserated with the guards when an escape forced them from their barracks into the woods. On a warm summer afternoon, when an American guard sat down, slumped against a tree, and dozed off, the Germans grew quiet to let him have his nap.[2]

A particular way in which work began to form a bond between the Americans and Germans involved animals. A good work horse brings as much satisfaction in America as in Germany, a bad one as much frustration. In the morning the horse drivers and a guard or two would go to the barn by Mill Brook to fetch the horses. Fifteen-year-old Donald Croteau would wave from the door of the house. The men would all wave back. A few of the Germans, who had learned enough English in school to converse with the Americans, would say "Good Morning!" Of the Americans in the camp and in the village, only the army interpreter spoke German. But the horses did better. They already had foreign language experience. A good twitch horse in the North Country had to understand commands in French as well as in English. It took little effort for them to learn German commands also, and Camp Stark produced a number of trilingual horses. They were common friends to Americans and Germans. Prisoner-of-war Willi Kiefer drove the horse for his work crew. One day the animal was injured in deep snow and had to be shot. Willi wept. The American foreman consoled him because he knew what it was like to lose a horse who had become a good friend.[3]

The work of Camp Stark did not remain the same for everyone, and its changes made new bonds between the Americans and the Germans. Not all the prisoners of war worked in the woods. Some worked on camp maintenance crews as mechanics, plumbers, carpenters, electricians, etc. Others were tailors, cobblers, barbers, cooks. Half a dozen Germans worked as cooks or in maintenance in the American side of Camp Stark. Working in a variety of circumstances with different American supervisors expanded the interaction between the two nationalities. Often the German craftsmen possessed the technical knowledge lacked by the Americans to accomplish a particular task. When a tractor became stuck, a German who had worked with tanks had it going in a few minutes. Unusual work could bring unusual camaraderie. On a cold winter day six prisoners of war and a guard were ordered to assist an army project on Mt. Washington, the highest peak in New England, notorious for its severe weather. The highest wind velocity ever measured, 231 miles per hour, had been clocked at the weather observatory on the summit of the mountain ten years before. The army needed to resupply fuel to an automatic weather station it maintained on the summit. The men from Camp Stark were given shovels to dig through the deep drifts on the upper ridges so the army snow vehicle could reach the summit. Once the drifts were behind them, the freezing guard handed his rifle to one of the prisoners and asked them all to climb in the cab and sit on him to warm him up as they crawled over the icy slopes to the top. The observatory crew welcomed them all inside, invited them to sit around the same table, fed them the same hot soup, and then waved them on their way down the mountain. Their experience made for a good story that night on both sides of Camp Stark.[4] Another unusual work assignment took a crew of prisoners of war and two guards to a Shelburne farm to put up hay for the Brown Company work horses. The Germans asked the guards to shoot woodchucks so they could cook them for dinner. The guards obliged, and the prisoners of war strung a dozen skinned woodchucks on a rope and carried them back to their kitchen.[5]

The woodchucks may have added variety to the German diet, but they were not necessary for nutrition. The Germans and Americans of Camp Stark shared good food and plenty of it. In 1944, all of them knew that their diet was better than that eaten by civilians in Germany—and in Stark. The usual working ration of 5,500 calories per man per day was checked periodically by the International Red Cross visits.[6] At first, the Germans and Americans ate similar food, but in the summer of 1944 the War Department, in the interest of food conservation, allowed menus to be altered to suit prisoner-of-war tastes, as long as the standard cost was not exceeded or the caloric level reduced.[7] Accordingly, Captain Kobus obtained rye flour, cabbage, turnips, and other food familiar to the Germans. They were encouraged to grow vegetables of their choice in their garden area. Kobus arranged for several whisky barrels to be donated so the Germans could make their own red cabbage sauerkraut. Then he made sure they sent some over to the American mess hall. The Germans were particularly fond of pork products, especially fatback. Lard sandwiches were their favorite, a taste that made the American guards cringe.[8] The German kitchen made the most of its food. At the end of the week they would leave just one barrel of garbage from 250 men. The American kitchen with only fifty guards to feed produced four or five barrels of waste.[9] Camp Stark made its single cameo appearance in the comprehensive German study of World War II prisoners of war in a brief report from the International Red Cross that carried the Germans' praise for their food at Camp Stark.[10] The prisoners of war at Stark, however, were not the only ones to benefit from a special menu. Sometimes the American dinner would be pork or ham. The German cook in the American kitchen, Helmut "Red" Mueller, would prepare something else for Sergeant Tausig, Austrian-born, a naturalized American, and Jewish. Said the German cook, "It's the least I can do."[11]

As the work, the war, and other factors began to connect rather than divide the Americans and Germans in Stark, they began to join together against outside forces. One of the strangest episodes involved the pursuit of military intelligence pertaining to ball-bearing factories in Germany. In 1944, the American air force made a strategic decision to attempt to cripple the Nazi war economy by bombing its ball-bearing factories. Without ball bearings, the American command assumed, the German war machine would screech to a halt. The Americans assigned highest priority in planes and personnel to this assault, mounting some of the most costly air raids of the war on either side. In connection with this operation, Captain Kobus was ordered to join all other prisoner-of-war camp commanders in the First Service Command (New England) at a special meeting in Boston. A visiting general explained to them the strategic decision and then told them that they could play a key role in the vital operation. No doubt, it was explained, some of their prisoners had lived in German towns in which there were ball-bearing factories. Camp commanders were told to obtain from their prisoners of war information about the location of such plants, using torture if necessary.[12]

Torture or other forms of coercion to obtain information were, of course, prohibited by the Geneva Convention, although in other prisoner-of-war camps and for other purposes American authorities bent or broke these regulations.[13] Kobus and others balked at the strange request, and eventually General Miles refused to have his officers comply unless the orders were placed in writing. The visiting general replied that was impossible, so the camp commanders were requested only to interview cooperative prisoners of war in order to obtain the information.[14] Some of the men of the 999 at Camp Stark, as well as anti-fascists in other camps, decided to assist the American fight against fascism by supplying some of the information sought.[15] It was a small episode, but it produced a strange alliance, first of the commander and his prisoners against the unorthodox request of the general, and then of the anti-Nazi prisoners and the American authorities in the bombing campaign against German war industry.

A less controversial form of collaboration or alliance between the army and the prisoners of war involved the familiar issue of the daily pulpwood quota. In the early period at Camp Stark, the army and the Brown Company blamed the prisoners of war for failure to meet the quota. The Germans were forced to produce or else lost canteen privileges or were sent to the small stockade. After the strike, they made up shortages by working on Sunday. However, this meant that the guards also were required to go to the woods on Sunday. Although there were weeks when this had to happen, the common interest of guards and prisoners encouraged them to cooperate as much as possible during the week in order to avoid Sunday work. Eventually, by Spring 1945, the army blamed production problems not on the prisoners of war, but on Brown Company policies and procedures.[16] In the course of everyday work, German military habits often occasioned goodwill in the Americans. The Germans were accustomed to standing and saluting when an American soldier entered their compound. As one guard said, "They made me, a corporal, feel like a general."[17]

As the war and the work began to establish a common community in Stark, with Germans and Americans allowing decency and cooperation to replace animosity and confrontation, other points of contact between the two national groups encouraged the growth of friendship. Most of these new opportunities for exchange were found in leisure activities. Such activities, at one time a mark of social distinction, have become a powerful force for social leveling in the Western world, bringing together people who are different in many ways. So it was in Stark. The increasing cordiality and cooperation that had grown out of their shared work environment involved most of the Germans but of the Americans only military personnel and civilian foremen. Family members of some of the Americans may have participated vicariously in these German-American relationships, but it was through shared leisure that the German-American circle of friendships widened to include the people of Stark village. They discovered, and later vowed to remember, how they and their German soldiers realized that they shared common interests, common culture, common humanity.

The War Department understood from the time the first prisoner of war arrived in the United States that everyone would have an easier time if the prisoners' free time were filled with appropriate recreation. Empty hours and the abrasion of time created explosive symptoms in prisoners: intense irritability, demoralizing melancholia, sudden anger. Recreation and intellectual diversion diffused potentially dangerous psychological and social tensions.[18] At Camp Stark, the political tension prevailing in some barracks made especially welcome recreational opportunities other than sitting around arguing politics or perhaps passing the time playing cards or chess.[19] Writing letters occupied evening hours for some. Geneva Convention regulations allowed prisoners of war to write two letters per week on special single-sheet prisoner-of-war stationery. Most did not write or receive that many letters—some only a few, some none—especially as postal service in Germany became irregular toward the end of the war. The letters traveled slowly, subject to censorship at both ends. Their contents were limited to noncontroversial issues, and most prisoners wrote about family concerns and offered general descriptions of their new countryside.[20] At first, American censors at Fort Devens perused Camp Stark mail, but eventually they realized that nothing of strategic value would reach the Nazi command from Camp

Stark, and then cursory censorship took place at the camp itself. It was rare and difficult for German prisoners of war in the United States to receive personal visitors, but one German in Stark was visited by an aunt, an American citizen living in Massachusetts.[21]

The canteen offered some diversion for the Germans. Using credit coupons earned by their labor, the prisoners of war were able to purchase cookies, candy, milk, toiletries, writing material, soda, cigarettes, and beer. The last two items were limited by a daily allowance. One time the prisoners made their own bootleg schnapps from potato peelings. They kept it hidden in the latrine until a few obviously inebriated prisoners of war caught the eye of the sergeant who then tracked down the potent brew and threw it away.[22] Although the canteen was inside the German compound, it influenced German-American friendships in three ways. The purchased snacks introduced the Germans to other elements of American culture; some acquired a taste for peanut butter candies that would be difficult to satisfy in the decades ahead. The abundant supply of cigarettes prompted German generosity to American civilians whose cigarette supply was rationed; when the prisoners of war saw their civilian foremen rolling their own cigarettes because of rationed regular brands, they often gave them packs they had bought in their canteen.[23] On a few occasions, the Germans would throw a carton over the fence into the snow on the other side, and a grateful foreman would pick it up.[24] Finally, the canteen allowed the Germans to obtain supplies for arts and crafts, which would form an important and enduring avenue of approach to the local population.

"Those prisoners were a talented bunch, I tell you," said former army guard Warren Hoyt, with an obvious touch of pride in having known them. "Each one of them had a special skill or trade he could do, first class."

Several of the captive Germans were accomplished artists who were delighted to share their work with the civilian foremen and army guards and through them with the people of the town. In pencil sketches, ink drawings, water colors and oil paintings, the prisoner-of-war artists left a rich and varied portfolio of their Camp Stark years. Some of the works were portraits, usually women, sketched from memory. Others recalled familiar scenes in Germany. Most expressed a sensitive visual appreciation of the artists' new North Woods world. Even forty years later, some of the most reflective and cherished paintings of the region hanging on living room walls from Colebrook to Conway are works by prisoner-of-war artists. Few of the surviving paintings and drawings from this politicized camp are political, although the camp commander prized his gift of a painting done on K-ration wrapping paper of a reluctant youth being "volunteered" in service to Hitler by Goering. Most paintings captured more peaceful subjects: birch trees and spruce stumps, lacy yellow autumn foliage, the buildings of Camp Stark with the gum-drop shaped Percy Peaks rising beyond. For army guard Carl Giordono, a sketch opened the way to his first friendship with a prisoner of war. During a break he noticed the prisoner hurriedly drawing and walked over to him. The artist looked at Giordono's name tag and began speaking to him in Italian. Detroit native Giordono happily picked up the conversation in Italian. The prisoner of war, an Austrian, handed the American soldier a sketch of himself in uniform, complete with rifle. The artist signed his name, Pagro; later, Giordono would feel pained to see him with his hands blistered from his axe.[25]

Communication in a language other than English or German formed the basis for other friendships. One of the prisoners of war, Georg Zeler, or really Georges Zéler, came from Klein Rosseln, or really Petite Rosselle, in Lorraine. A jovial lad of seventeen or eighteen, Zéler would chatter at length in French with the French-Canadian foremen. Another foreman was a Norwegian, from one of Berlin's Scandinavian ethnic groups who came to work in the forests and brought ski-jumping from their homeland to the United States. He found two prisoners of war who spoke his mother tongue with whom he formed special friendships.

Handicrafts proved even more effective than paintings in forming friendships between Germans and Americans in Stark. Like the paintings, the objects crafted by Germans found their way into many New Hampshire homes. At the very beginning, when more tension than decency marked German-American relations, a few of the prisoners took advantage of some

American guards. After somehow obtaining silver dollars through illicit commercial exchange, the Germans fashioned them into rings, on which they would engrave *Afrika Korps* ensignia. They would then sell them back to the Americans as authentic German souvenirs.[26] Later, handicraft items were given rather than sold, in a spirit of friendship rather than avarice. The items the Americans sought most enthusiastically were matchstick houses and ships-in-bottles. Also highly prized were knives fashioned from old saw blades with handles made from deer antlers found in the woods. Most prison camps did not allow their inmates to make knives.

Handicrafts played a special role in the development of German-American accord in Stark because camp-made toys were often given by the Germans to American youngsters with whom they became acquainted. Few forces bring people together more effectively than common love for children. The prisoners of war viewed with special affection the children who reminded them of their own offspring or siblings back home in Germany. Sons and daughters of Brown Company foremen came to the American side of the camp with their fathers. Sometimes they brought their friends to walk by the German camp. One of the German cooks in the American kitchen always gave shoulder rides around the mess hall. "For the little girl," or "For your son," the Germans would say as they pressed a gift into American hands: an Easter basket woven from birch bark, a tiny chair, a hobby horse, a little sled carved for Christmas, toys, and trinkets. The gifts endured and are now being passed on to the children's children.

American wives and girlfriends received special attention from "Red" Mueller and other German cooks. Sunday dinner in the American mess was the social event of the week. The German kitchen staff, scrubbed clean, dressed in white coats, towel over the arm, would serve as waiters. "Red" was the German whom all the servicemen knew best. He cooked their favorite dishes for them on Sundays, and sometimes put out something special for special people, not only for Sgt. Tausig, but also, for example, for Dr. Foster's wife. She had taught him how to make donuts.[27] He joked in French with the French-Canadian girls. Years later, the wives were still saying that nobody ever made as much fuss over them as did "Red" and the other German cooks.

Religion brought some Americans and Germans together, although Camp Stark was not a particularly religious place. The unusually high percentage of Marxists in the 999 diminished the role of religion. Nonetheless, religious services were held. The Geneva Convention affirmed religious freedom for prisoners of war and allowed either internal clergymen or outside clergymen to conduct regular worship services. From the beginning, American clergymen played a role at Camp Stark. Robert Sharp, a Methodist minister in nearby Groveton, spoke at the camp every other Sunday. At first he had some problems. The 999 men put pressure on the Normandy captives not to attend church. Or they encouraged nonreligious people to go for the sole purpose of obtaining whatever gifts the pastor and his assistant might bring. Going to church to get rather than to give happened in many prisoner-of-war camps. American chaplains who counted heads and not motives overestimated their appeal. [28] Reverend Sharp was suspicious of his smirking translator, and his rudimentary German confirmed that the initial words "I come to you as God's messenger," instead became "I come to you as an evil messenger."

The minister had trouble with some Americans, also. Not all Groveton Methodists wanted their pastor to preach at the camp. Sharp's congregation had already become disturbed earlier when he had spoken against the American government's incarceration of Japanese-Americans, and in his sermon had praised a prominent Japanese Christian. His preaching to the Germans raised some hackles higher. Less than a year after starting Protestant services at Camp Stark, Sharp left his Groveton church. He took with him a painting done by a prisoner of war thankful for his ministry. Portraying a rustic German house, it was entitled "Home", and for many years hung over the mantle in Sharp's home, his most cherished possession. [29]

Father Heon, the Catholic priest from Groveton, enjoyed a smoother ministry at Camp Stark. The prisoners of war constructed a little chapel in one of their rooms, for which Captain Kobus procured an altar cloth. A small group of both Catholics and Protestants attended the weekly service. Protestant Ger-

hard Clauss, the slender young German whose English earned
him the job of clerk, played the portable organ that Father Heon
brought along. One day a 17-year-old altar boy who accompanied the priest slipped Clauss a donut and some wine taken
from the priest's cabinet. Clauss shared it with his two compan-
ions.[30] The young German and the priest kept in touch for a few
years after the war. Forty years later, Clauss learned that Father
Heon had died, and was buried in Canada. He located the
former altar boy and wrote to him:

> Whenever you are in front of Father Heon's grave, please say a
> prayer on my behalf. . . . In spite of all the political situation
> against Germany in those days, he developed human relations to
> us and kept them even in the dark days. . . . His personal courage
> and sympathy for us will be unforgotten by me.[31]

In spite of the prevailing leftist sentiment against religion in
Camp Stark, religious contacts formed a small but unbreakable
bond between some Germans and Americans. Furthermore,
the role of religion in sustaining German-American friendships
continued to grow even after Camp Stark closed because of the
respect given to Father Heon in the local community.

A more obvious German-American connection formed in
music. Classical works as well as popular tunes reminded Germans and Americans of their common culture. Their music
came live and recorded. Through the combination of the Red
Cross and profits from the canteen, the prisoners of war purchased musical instruments, a victrola, and some records. They
were able to establish a small orchestra with violins, guitars,
and a piano. They played occasional concerts to which they
invited the American officers; Captain Kobus and Lieutenant
A. Jaillet attended from time to time.[32] More regular music
came with the Sunday morning record concerts, usually Beethoven, piped over the public address system by American Sgt.
Tausig. Prisoner-of-war Wenzel was charged with changing
these records every Sunday, often eight or nine records for a
symphony. The record concerts served to bring together the
Americans and Germans in two ways. There were those on
both sides who showed appreciation of Beethoven. And on both
sides there was shared distaste among those who did not.[33]

Although sport, rather than reducing international political tensions, has more often reflected or even magnified them, there have been times of reconciliation through athletics, perhaps most often on a small scale. Camp Stark was too small to have much of an athletics program. Sometimes on hot days 5 or 6 guards would take about 30 prisoners of war to a swimming hole on the river so they could swim for an hour, although this served to cool them off more than to promote exercise. Soccer games formed the principal athletic program at the camp. The Germans set up a small soccer field along the fence on the northeast side of their compound. They divided themselves into teams and played enthusiastically on Sunday afternoons. At first the Americans remained spectators. The guards watched and sometimes cheered them on from the adjacent watchtowers.[34] One day First Sergeant Frank Chappell organized a soccer game between guards and prisoners of war. It was all to be in good fun, but guards were guards and prisoners were prisoners, and the guards had decided before it even began that they had to win. In the course of the game, Chappell explained later, he collided with one of the leading German players, accidently kicking him. Automatically, the American sergeant apologized. The German looked at him quizzically, surprised. Then they both smiled and played on. At that moment, Chappell said, it was as though a crust broke. There was no longer that strange feeling between them. Natural instincts of sport and decency took over. "The prisoners slaughtered us," he said with a laugh.[35]

Pets formed part of the Camp Stark population, and they also did their part to bring Americans and Germans together. Although most of the pets lived in the German compound, some of them wandered back and forth across the road between the German and American sides of the camp: kittens and cats, puppies and dogs. The Germans found most of their pets while working in the woods: squirrels, snakes, chipmunks, and a raccoon. One prisoner of war kept a rabbit, and then found it a mate. When the rabbit population reached thirty, he was forced to let them go, although he cried as he did.[36] Jacob was the pet crow whose broken wing kept him from flying high or far. The Germans painted "PW" on his back, and turned him into the camp clown. He hopped or flew between the American and German sides, depending on where he could receive the most hand-outs. He teased dogs, cats, and raccoons by pecking them on the rump and then flying away. Shiny objects, even inside buildings, fell prey to his heists. More than one American watch or set of keys disappeared, perhaps taken over to the German side. Americans and Germans alike whiled away time watching Jacob's antics. Finally, there was the bear cub. A German woods crew shook a tree, and out of its top fell a small bear. They wrapped it in their coats, took it back to the camp, and tamed it so it would follow them around. Americans and Germans posed together for snapshots with the bear. One day it disappeared. Some guards thought they saw the mother bear dig under the fence to retrieve the little one.

For more formal entertainment, the Germans and Americans had the same choices. Much of it continued the process of exposing the Germans to American culture. Every seven or ten days a movie would come to camp, typical Hollywood fare of the 1930s. Sometimes the feature films would be accompanied by standard newsreels. Although World War II newsreels were infused with American propaganda, some of the Germans were surprised by their frankness, especially when they depicted American casualties, as in footage of the battle of Monte Cassino.[37] German troops did not suffer casualties on film. Other news came in magazines and newspapers. The Germans were permitted to read any American periodical, the cost of subscription being met from canteen profits. The *New York Times, Boston Globe, Boston Post, Berlin* (N.H.) *Reporter, Look,* and *Time* were read by Germans and Americans.[38] Prisoners of war in larger camps were able to publish their own weekly newspapers, often running to more than ten pages. Copies of these journals from Fort Devens and Camp Houlton sometimes found their way to Camp Stark. Once in a while, the Stark prisoners of war would mimeograph a longhand newsletter.[39] Other reading material included works by German authors like Franz Werfel and Thomas Mann, made available through the Y.M.C.A. Northern New Hampshire was never known for its rich radio programming. The Germans preferred a Montreal station and claimed greater objectivity for Canadian news of the war. The

French-Canadian radio station played European music familiar to German ears, including Christmas choruses in French
and German.[40]

As leisure activities afforded more opportunities for German-
American contact, a new openness developed between the two
groups, which allowed bonds to be formed not only through
sharing common interests but also through perceiving cultural
differences. They reached the stage of cultural exchange when
cultural differences were no longer baffling, not yet frustrating,
but merely intriguing.

The village and the camp were brought closer together by
another shared attribute, their small size. Neither the village nor
the camp enjoyed the amenities of larger towns or larger camps.
So they became accustomed to making do with less, providing
their own entertainment, being satisfied with what was
available.

Camp Stark's small size denied its prisoners of war the formal
educational opportunities offered in larger camps. Eventually
the American education program became the most popular of
all recreational activities in prisoner-of-war camps. Inmate
instructors, correspondence courses, and even extension
courses offered by American universities gave prisoners of war
in large camps a curriculum that included courses in almost
every academic discipline and technical field. The prisoner-of-
war camp education program assumed such large dimensions
that, in a strange step for the middle of a war, in May 1944 the
Reich Ministry of Education published a detailed plan by which
prisoners of war in American camp curricula would receive
high school and university credit for their studies.[41] Without
these options, Camp Stark made do on its own. Some of the
prisoners of war at Stark taught foreign language courses.
Georges Zéler taught French and English to Willi Volz, a
Dutchman who, like Zéler, was a non-German somehow caught
up in the German army. Gerhard Clauss learned Russian from
one of the communists in the 999. In turn, Clauss taught cal-
culus to a few fellow-captives.[42] Sergeant Tausig, the Austrian-
born American army interpreter, taught an evening course in
American history and democracy to interested prisoners of
war.[43] These courses, elementary though they might have been,

served to provide needed intellectual diversion and growth for those who felt cut off from the world of learning. One man assured his family back in Germany that learning American history kept his mind alert, and that even though a prisoner of war he "was still a cultured man."[44]

A controversial and initially secret companion to the education program was the re-education program. As soon as the struggle between the Nazis and the anti-Nazis in the prisoner-of-war camps became known, persons in the press, the military service and academic circles demanded that the War Department do something for and with the anti-Nazis and other politically impressionable prisoners. Several proposals reached the Provost Marshal General's office, all requesting some form of democratic instruction or indoctrination for appropriate prisoners of war. Carefully reasoned arguments stressed the importance of using German prisoners of war re-educated in democratic principles to form the vanguard of a democratic post-war German society.[45] The proposals apparently fell on deaf ears, being termed "inadvisable."[46] Once again, the Geneva Convention seemed to dictate action, or inaction. Captor governments were not to subject prisoners of war to political propaganda or re-education (what would later be termed "brain washing"). The U.S. government wanted to protect American prisoners in Germany from Nazi re-education and propaganda.

Actually the War Department had already adopted a secret plan to skirt the Geneva Convention through the provision of allowing "intellectual diversion" to set up a re-education program. To avoid German reprisal, it was highly classified. Complaints continued to appear in the press while the army secretly began re-educating anti-Nazi prisoners of war. The first efforts focused on secret schools in Rhode Island, where carefully screened prisoners of war were trained for administrative and police positions in the government of postwar Germany.

After V-E Day, a broader re-education program was instituted, aimed not only at anti-Nazis but also at non-Nazi prisoners of war thought to be receptive to democratic ideas. The program, organized at Fort Eustis, Virginia, sent thousands of prisoners of war en route to Germany through a six-day course in democracy. They heard lectures and participated in discussions designed to educate them about American and German democratic traditions. Six days was not much time in which to make up for their nearly complete ignorance of Western democratic history and of German history before 1933.[47]

The Fort Eustis re-education program, nicknamed "the six-day bicycle race," attempted to train over 23,000 returning prisoners of war to become a spearhead of democracy in Germany.[48] It is impossible to tell how well it worked.[49] Some, especially the proven anti-Nazis, took part enthusiastically. But not all those who participated were anti-Nazi. Some were camouflaged Nazis seeking a quick ticket home. Others energetically embraced the freedom of democratic life. Eventually West Germany became a democratic society. Many of the 23,000 Fort Eustis graduates wove themselves into important public and private positions in the fabric of that society. Perhaps there was a connection.

Camp Stark sent a number of its Germans back home through the Fort Eustis program. The anti-fascists in the 999 as well as younger captives were prime candidates for intense exposure to democratic ideas and methods. For example, escapee Franz Bacher, the former Camp Stark resident who had already demonstrated his appreciation for a democratic society by his weeks of freedom in Manhattan, was reunited at Fort Eustis with his accomplice at Stark who had stayed behind. They and others from Camp Stark, upon completion of the Fort Eustis program, were offered administrative positions with the American military government. Most declined. They wanted to play a role in a free society, but only enough to live their private lives.

The prisoners of war in Stark, especially the former inmates in 999, had been removed from society for a long time. Once in Stark, they rarely glimpsed American society, except when driving through the tiny village on the way to the work site. A severe medical problem could take a prisoner of war to Berlin, but that was a rare event. Most medical problems could be treated right at the camp. The German medic, Johann Jarclovski, helped the cause of German-American friendship. The Americans came to prefer him to some of their own physicians.

During the last months of the camp, he and Dr. Foster formed a competent and respected medical team. Jarclovski was permitted to travel in the doctor's truck to make unofficial "rounds" in the village. Sometimes he would bring some helpers to fill the Foster's woodshed or wash their floors—anything to get out of camp for a while.[50]

Jarclovski's story was a tragic one. He spoke English because he had lived in New York City in the mid-1930s and worked as a medic for the fire department. He returned to Germany to fetch his wife and his child in 1939. The war caught him and he eventually landed in the 999, probably for socialist activity either before or after his return. He had heard nothing from his family, who lived next to the Hamburg railway station, and held little hope for their survival. The Americans said he was a good medic, better than any doctor. But they said he always looked sad.[51]

When an injury or illness was severe enough to require hospitalization for a prisoner, usually at the St. Louis Hospital in Berlin, this always proved to be an exciting event for the hospital staff. A German prisoner of war on the ward was more than a curiosity, however. He provided an opportunity for something deeper. Three of the prisoners of war who were treated there were deeply moved by the attention they received from the sisters who worked at the Catholic hospital and even from strangers. One, laid up with an injured foot, was moved to tears when women, mothers of sons at war, brought flowers and candy, because "young men are the same everywhere."[52]

Dentistry followed the same pattern as medicine: camp treatment first, then to Berlin. The prisoner-of-war dental technician was not as popular as the medic. He was clever enough to fashion a silver crown with very rudimentary tools, but his equipment was primitive. For extractions, the "anesthesia" amounted to being tied down with towels. His drill was turned by prisoner-of-war pedal power.[53] Finally, the camp authorities assigned most dental work to Berlin, thus providing still one more way for Germans to meet the larger American community. Normally, facing tooth extraction in downtown Berlin would not beckon as a pleasant experience. Yet a diary entry written by a German prisoner of war in June 1944, even before there was much friendship between Germans and Americans at Camp Stark, gives a glimpse into the mind of the captive:

> Usually going to the dentist is a painful experience, but this time it would be a pleasant interlude. Six of us were driven to the town [Berlin] to get our teeth pulled. It was a welcome glance into civilian life. We looked down the streets from the windows of the waiting room with longing. There were mostly women, few men, only a few children. We longed for civilian life. We all wished that once again we could walk on the street without a guard, wherever we wanted to go.[54]

Many of the Stark village civilians desired to extend friendship toward the Camp Stark Germans sooner than they were permitted. The Sunday drives included more of the sympathetic, fewer of the curious. Occasionally, civilians walked up to the gate, some with socks or other small items to give to the prisoners of war, but regulations forbidding this exchange were at first enforced. Later, things relaxed. Motives for the proffered acts of kindness may have been simple sympathy for incarcerated young men, perhaps something like the feeling portrayed in the poignant scene from Jean Renoir's classic film on World War I prisoners of war, *Grand Illusion,* when elderly German women stand outside the camp and say sadly, *"armen Jungen,"* ("poor boys"). But it is more likely that the desire for friendship was based on the concern beginning to focus that enemies become friends, that Germans and Americans live in peace, at least in our village.

An unusual comparison indicates that the mere problem of detention in New Hampshire was not always enough to engender expressions of sympathy or friendship. Camp Stark was not New Hampshire's only World War II incarceration camp. There were four small camps for conscientious objectors, also using former C.C.C. facilities. The American conscientious objectors were not treated as well by the civilians living near their camps as were the German prisoners of war. People shunned and repudiated the American men in the C.O. camps while they made overtures of friendship to enemy prisoners of war.[55] The friendship that the people of Stark began to extend to the Camp Stark Germans was based not only on their common decency but also on their interest in representatives of a different culture and their undefined but sincere hopes for peace and accord between nations.

By early 1945, a few people realized that something special was happening in Stark. Most did not perceive this, even though they were part of it. The decency and even friendship that grew between Germans and Americans was not planned, not without set-back, not unanimously approved. Often it just happened, shaped by working together, shared space and time, wartime social changes, common recreational interests, the smile of a child. A small number on both sides either fostered the friendships actively with the zeal of social crusaders or avoided contact as strictly as possible with the other group. More were open but circumspect, tentative at first, then cordial, finally relaxed in their unexpected international relationships. The Camp Stark German-American friendship grew slowly and haltingly. Eventually, after months, years, or even decades, as it assumed increasing importance in the minds of those who recalled it, it gave significance to young lives, older lives, and even to the costly war out of which it had emerged. As the people of Camp Stark pondered this strange product of World War II, they sought to make this result of those low and terrible times serve a higher and better purpose.

Camp Stark had a favorite song. One day some of the guards were humming "Don't Fence Me In" at the camp gate. Gerhard Clauss asked what it was. The guards told him the title and taught him the words. The next morning all the Germans were singing it, in German and English. Forty years later, during an elegantly catered dinner in the Stark Town Hall, former prisoners of war and their families, former guards and their families, former civilian foremen and their families, and the people of Stark all linked arms and sang "Don't Fence Me In." There wasn't a dry eye in the hall.

7

Peace and Despair

As winter's snows melted into spring 1945 the decent equilibrium between the Germans and Americans in Stark was threatened by stress from forces beyond the camp. The fragile faith placed in each other by Germans and Americans, tested severely, sometimes wavered but eventually endured. The first year of Camp Stark saw anger and acrimony give way gradually to acceptance and accord. The second year, especially for the Germans, became an emotional roller coaster powered by uneasiness about an uncomfortable past, confusion about an uncertain present, and worry about an unknown future.

The general settling down of the patterns of work and relaxation at Camp Stark had brought a sense of stability and peace. The developing cooperation among prisoners of war, civilian foremen, and army guards made everyone's life a little easier. The gestures of goodwill between people of the village and the Germans brought needed confirmation of human decency and dignity. Not everyone was happy all the time. There was still a war going on, and anxiety hung in the air. Still crowded together, the Germans chafed under their indefinite incarceration. Tensions flared in the camp from time to time. Political strife remained the most likely cause, but those were days when anything could lead to trouble: bullying, bickering, the homosexual activity common to all prisons—even an individual prisoner singing off-key. Confinement caused not only irritability but also unpredictability; the same provocation could lead to rage one day, laughter the next. The stress got to some people. One afternoon at the work site a prisoner of war put down his axe and began to walk away acros a field. The guard yelled "Halt," but the prisoner of war kept walking. As the guard placed ammunition in his rifle and raised it to fire a shot, the other Germans began to shout at their wandering comrade who suddenly stopped and came back to work, his tension apparently relieved.[1]

The winter had ended escape attempts for the time being, but with the return of warmer weather the sense of adventure called. An Austrian prisoner of war encouraged a young 18-year-old from East Prussia to join him in a trip away from the camp. They slipped off from work and hid in the forest. After spending a day in a hunting camp that they discovered, they put on civilian clothes found there and headed for the railroad, which they heard in the distance. They hopped a freight train, but at the next station were questioned by American soldiers who refused to believe their story that they were Dutch sailors. After a phone call to Camp Stark, both men were on their way back. The 18-year-old was put in the little stockade for ten days, on a bread-and-coffee diet. But by now the Germans had figured how to keep small amounts of food hidden in the stockade. After the young prisoner of war had his head shaved to mark him as an escapee, half a dozen of his friends shaved their heads in sympathy.[2] Since it was determined that the older Austrian had lured in a younger man to attempt escape, the Austrian was sent away to Camp Houlton, in northern Maine.

In May 1945, an administrative change designated Camp Stark as a branch camp of Camp Houlton rather than Fort Devens. The only impact of this change was felt by some trouble-makers, both prisoners of war and guards. Earlier, being transferred back to comfortable Fort Devens was hardly a punishment. Being banished to the potato fields of Houlton was. Guards who neglected their duty were sent to Houlton as quickly as unruly prisoners. One small group of prisoners suddenly shipped to Camp Houlton in 1945 was the handful of S.S. soldiers who had been mistakenly assigned to Stark in late 1944. The camp commander did not realize that his camp held these men from the S.S., although anti-Nazis in the camp quickly learned their identity. Not until 1945 did he receive orders to check his prisoners of war for the tell-tale arm tattoo.[3]

In April 1945, as it became increasingly clear that the war in Europe was in its final stages, several shocking events made their impact on Camp Stark, an impact different than in most German prisoner-of-war camps. First came the death of President Roosevelt on April 12. The tragic news from Warm Springs took the people in Stark and everywhere else by surprise. Americans were stunned by the loss of the man who had been president as long as many could remember. In German prisoner-of-war camps, especially those dominated by Nazis, FDR's death seemed a stroke of good fortune, perhaps signaling the breakup of the strange coalition of the United States, the Soviet Union, and Great Britain, which had waged war against Hitler's Reich. Things were different at Camp Stark. The prisoners of war were silent and sad, as if experiencing a personal loss. When their spokesman and a delegation presented a letter of condolence from the Germans to Captain Kobus, they were close to tears.[4] Two and a half weeks later, when Hitler's death was announced, the Germans at Camp Stark displayed no emotion. A few of the younger ones who clung to their Nazi upbringing refused to believe it, but most men at Camp Stark, especially the anti-fascist majority, seemed relieved by the removal of one more obstacle to the war's end and their return home.[5]

In all, the news of the deaths of the leaders of the United States and Germany did not have as much impact as the news of other deaths being reported from Europe: the millions who perished in the Nazi extermination camps. The Nazi atrocities and the appropriate response to the Nazi atrocities form a part of the story of the 20th century with which the world is still attempting to cope. Who knew and did what, how much, and when are questions too large even to be reviewed here. The War Department decided that films of the extermination camps and other Nazi atrocities would be mandatory viewing for all German prisoners of war in the United States. Officials intended the films to drive home a sense of collective guilt and also to support the re-education program. In each camp, the films were ordered shown under the same conditions: all prisoners of war were forced to attend, silence had to be maintained during the film, no discussion afterwards was permitted. The response of German prisoners of war in camps throughout America to the films varied. A few recoiled in horror, destroyed their German uniforms, and even took up collections for concentration camp survivors. Another group disbelieved the pictures, dismissing the films as clumsy American or even Russian propaganda.[6] Most German prisoners of war were shocked and depressed by the films, though wondering why they had been shown to them. Self-exoneration was the most common response: "Why did they show that to *us?* We didn't do it."[7] The films did not further the concept of collective guilt among the prisoners of war. They felt they had no connection with what had happened in the extermination camps.[8]

At Camp Stark, however, the reaction was unusual. Camp authorities followed the standard procedures for showing the films, and had to drag at least one reluctant German who did not wish to see what his countrymen had done.[9] Most of the Normandy prisoners of war at Camp Stark were, in the words of one, "astonished and shamed" by what they saw in the films, and since many of them were teenagers or barely in their twenties, they professed neither involvement nor knowledge of the camps.[10] But Camp Stark men from the 999 claimed to know all too much about the camps. Some of them had served terms as inmates in concentration camps. Rather than professing disbelief or ignorance, their attitude was more "We told you so!"

Revelation of the horror of the Nazi atrocities changed American public opinion about German prisoners of war. In late 1944 and early 1945, as the prisoner-of-war program began to run smoothly, as prisoner-of-war labor proved helpful in so many ways to the American war effort, as Americans became accustomed to German prisoners of war, fears and concern about coddling faded. Some Americans began to befriend German prisoners of war. The American government and people knew they were supposed to distinguish between the Nazis and the German people. After all, the Germans had been the Nazi's first victims. But now images of the concentration camps blurred this distinction. Many Americans demanded that all Germans be blamed for the atrocities. In prisoner-of-war camps all across the United States incarcerated Germans felt the wave of judgment, recrimination, and hatred. At about the same time, problems with food supply suddenly resurrected the coddling issue. Even though the war in Europe seemed close to its end, the United States was preparing itself for a protracted struggle in the Pacific. Food supplies, especially meats, were increasingly reserved for the armed forces. The public began to demand that the prisoners of war be among the first to feel the pinch.[11] Complaints from America's war-ravaged British ally that German prisoners were eating better than British civilians inflamed the issue.[12] Then, as a war-weary, rationed, indignant, and angry America began to call for harsh treatment and even punishment for all Germans, the major protection for the German prisoners of war disappeared.

When Germany surrendered officially to the Allies on May 8, 1945, the primary reason for proper treatment of German prisoners of war in the United States no longer pertained. All along, the War Department had insisted that its objective was to obtain proper treatment of the American prisoners of war in German hands. Now these were all liberated, and the Nazi regime vanquished. This simple but important change, in addition to the aroused anti-German sentiment of American public opinion, let the axe fall on German prisoners of war in the United States. Immediately after V-E Day, their food rations were cut, their canteen privileges curtailed, their work quota increased.[13]

At Camp Stark, the new policy came as a bitter blow. The daily food ration was reduced from 5,500 to 1,800 calories; the canteen no longer sold beer, milk, cigarettes, or candy; and the wood quota was raised to over one cord. In prisoner-of-war camps all across the United States there was disappointment and anger at the change in American policy, which most prisoners interpreted as childish revenge. Perhaps the Nazi propagandists had been right about the American character. At Camp Stark the attitude was one of discouragement, a sense of betrayal, and renewed fears of a fascist America. The anti-fascists in the camp had trouble abandoning their persistent fears about resurgent German fascism or American fascism lurking beneath the surface of American military behavior. They began to despair of America's ability to teach democracy to Germany.[14] A visit from the International Red Cross representative at the end of May noted the precipitous decline in German morale. Part of this was attributed to prisoner anxiety about families in Germany and the complete absence of communication in the last months of the war. Concern was also expressed over a recent press report indicating that officers and Nazi prisoners of war might be the first to be shipped back to Germany. But the primary source of complaint was the reduced food ration. The International Red Cross report concluded that the ration was inadequate for men performing the labor expected at Camp Stark.[15]

The post-VE Day regulations brought the camp to the brink of a second strike. A major work stoppage was averted through the intervention of Sgt. Tausig and the avowed stance of Captain Kobus. As always, Kobus considered first the camp's pulpwood quota, and he realized that undernourished men would be unable to meet their daily quota. He assured the prisoners of war of his own opposition to the new diet and vowed his best effort to have the former ration renewed. Camp commanders are not usually regarded as humanitarians, but the Germans knew how dedicated the captain was to sufficient pulpwood production. So they resumed work, hoping that Kobus would make good on his promises to increase the rations. When his immediate protests fell on deaf ears at First Service Command headquarters, Kobus began to weigh each prisoner daily and to keep track of both production and accidents. Within a few weeks the average prisoner had lost fifteen to twenty pounds. The weakened prisoners suffered an increase of accidents in the woods, and their production lagged. Finally, during one of General Miles' visits to Stark, Kobus persuaded him to give a verbal order to resume the former ration. It took nearly two and a half months before many prisoners of war regained the weight they had lost.[16]

Meanwhile, in the midst of their bad times, the German prisoners of war at Stark heard news that brought them additional concern, and even fear. Some new guards were coming to the camp who might make things very tough on the Germans. These new guards had just returned to the United States after months of suffering as prisoners of war in Germany. One way the War Department met the renewed charges of coddling was to announce the decision to assign newly liberated American prisoners of war to serve out their military duty by guarding Germans. "These men," the announcement assured an American public increasingly irate about the treatment its own soldiers had received in Germany, "who have experienced captivity and detention by the enemy, are considered to be eminently qualified for these duties."[17] The implied threat of vengeance was clear.

The American former prisoners of war assigned to guard duty at Stark had emerged from the horrors of the Bad Orb prisoner-of-war camp east of Frankfurt. Captured during the Battle of the Bulge, these men had marched without food for four days from Belgium to Germany. Then they had endured a four-day rail journey locked in a box car with sixty men without food or water. A final 3-mile march took them to Bad Orb where for the next hundred days they subsisted on grass soup with a few potatoes. One man's weight dropped to ninety-seven pounds.[18]

The arrival of these men at Camp Stark brought one of the camp's great surprises. The former American prisoners of war bore no animosity toward the German prisoners of war at Camp Stark. Instead, the closest friendships were formed between Germans and Americans who shared the prisoner-of-war experience. Several reasons lay behind these unexpected friendships. To begin with, the Americans brought first-hand news of the situation in Germany. It may have been bad news about a devastated country and suffering civilians but at least it was reliable news. Secondly, the Americans empathized with the plight of the German prisoners of war. Revenge against the Germans in Stark would do nothing to diminish the suffering they had endured in Germany. They had seen enough suffering, punishment, and hatred. So, when the Germans' rations were cut in May 1945, these American guards slipped food and cigarettes to the Germans, assuring them that they did not support the new American policy.[19] Finally, the Germans discovered that the Americans who had returned from Germany would talk to them in ways that were deeper and more understanding. One German prisoner explained, "They even spoke a little German, and they played football with us."[20] Another

Camp Stark German said of former American prisoners of war like Walton, Brax, and Wyman, "These people were of great help to us, and they were more 'comrades' than guards. They often were a big comfort to us."[21]

The new guards who had been prisoners of war helped to set a new tone in the guard-prisoner relationship at Camp Stark. Although there were standing orders prohibiting fraternization, the discussions between the guards and the prisoners lengthened and deepened. The Germans felt that the new American guards had acquired a "European outlook," that their experience in Europe, terrible as it had been, had exposed them to European perspectives on the war, on politics, on history, on time, on life, in ways that eluded most American G.I.s. Some of the Germans at Stark had attempted from time to time to discuss with interested Americans the social, economic, and political conditions in Germany and Europe that had formed the breeding ground for fascism and war. They concluded that the parochial political and life experiences of most American guards kept them from grasping what had happened in Germany in the 1920s and 1930s.[22] But the new guards' traumatic European experience enlarged their view of the human condition, enabling a common comprehension to emerge from the conversations between Americans and Germans. Each side felt more understood by the other.

Camp Stark weathered the crisis caused by the post-VE Day changes better than did most camps. The new friendships between Americans and Germans were stretched but not severed. The new restrictions from Washington were another outside force that, although borne by the Germans, in some ways brought the entire Camp Stark community closer together. There may have been a few guards and civilians who were not concerned if the prisoners of war ate less and worked more. But to most of the community it did not seem fair. They knew that a man who cuts pulpwood had to eat right.

By early autumn life had improved for the prisoners. The diet had improved, though more in terms of nutrition than taste. Once again milk was sold in the canteen, although beer never reappeared. It had been difficult for the Germans and Americans alike at Camp Stark to keep general feelings of animosity directed toward each other's government from intruding on private relationships. There were times when the best intentions failed, and feelings became bruised. But usually an unspoken commitment to decency, fairness, and even friendship sustained the relationships which they had formed. As Christmas rolled around again, the second Camp Stark Christmas, homemade Christmas cards and presents were exchanged. It was the first peacetime Christmas in five years for the Americans, but the Germans were still prisoners of war. Many thoughts clouded their future.

Anxiety about family members in Germany became oppressive and corrosive for many. Word from Germany after the end of the war came irregularly. News could be weeks or months old when it arrived. Some had not heard from or about their relatives or friends for a year or more. Others already knew that there was no one in Germany to whom they would return. Many wondered where they would return as well as when they would return. The partition of Germany into Allied occupation zones became the most discussed issue inside the camp. In late 1945 and early 1946 few people imagined the future evolution of two separate German states. But many questions and real concerns plagued those whose homes lay in the Russian sector. The only answers lay in rumors, which flew continually at the camp among the Germans, among the Americans, between the two: The camp would close in a few weeks. The camp would remain open until the Brown Company could hire enough civilians. Repatriation would begin next week, next month, next year. Anti-Nazis would be sent home first. Nazis would return first to Germany to work in coal mines. German prisoners of war would be assigned to reconstruction projects in France, Belgium, and Great Britain. German prisoners of war would be shipped as laborers to the Soviet Union.

What would happen the next day always seemed certain, however: they would be working in the woods somewhere around Stark. For some it had become a routine that was now almost easy. An energetic crew of five young men working in a good stand of trees might have their quota stacked by early afternoon and be able to snooze in the sun for a few hours. Others poked along, never working any harder than necessary, perhaps enjoying the fresh air, just barely reaching their quota. A few struggled through every day, hating every minute of the life of a woodcutter. The return of cold weather and the grip of winter made life uncomfortable for guard and prisoner alike, linking them together against their snowy adversary. The deep snows of the new year brought a sobering reminder that theirs was dangerous work, as death came to the forest.

Failure to meet their daily quota sent work crews back to the woods on a Sunday morning in February 1946. As they worked to fell a tree, a dead portion broke off, striking 19-year-old Nowak Dow on the back of the head, killing him instantly. The young victim's body was taken to a funeral home in Berlin, and then to the prisoner-of-war cemetery at Fort Devens.[23] The accident at first numbed the camp and then led to recrimination. A few people, Americans and Germans, said the victim had simply made the unfortunate mistake, generally avoided by woodcutters, of standing too close. Others insisted that no one should have been ordered to work that snowy day because on the previous evening all the Germans had received an inoculation that had produced side effects including fever and weak, sore muscles. They blamed the American authorities for the tragedy. The young man, these people claimed, was too weak to move away from the falling tree.[24] Among some of the villagers an erroneous rumor persisted that the young German had been driven by prison confinement to commit suicide.

There were two other deaths associated with Camp Stark, both involving Americans, neither work-related. In mid-1944 the body of an American sergeant was discovered between the latrine and the barracks. He apparently died of natural causes, although inebriation may have played a role in his death.[25] During the second winter, a young Stark woman died of carbon monoxide poisoning in a car parked near the camp with its engine running all night. Her companion, a young American serviceman stationed at Camp Stark, survived only because the window on his side of the car was broken, allowing some air to enter. The state police acted perhaps too aggressively, questioning even the Germans inside the camp until the camp commander persuaded the police that the accident should be attributed to the loneliness and temptations of wartime.[26]

By 1946, wartime was over. Camp Stark's days were numbered, although no one seemed to know the number. After VE Day, and certainly after the surrender of the Japanese in September, neither the Germans nor the Americans of Camp Stark would have imagined the place would still be operating in 1946. By now the people of the village had grown accustomed to the prisoner-of-war camp in their town, and they had grown proud of it. When they thought about it, they were proud of themselves, too, of the way they had adjusted to it all, of the way they had made friends with some of the foreigners. The Germans focused their thoughts on going home, picking up their lives again. But their thoughts would come back to the New Hampshire village that had been their home, or at least where they had lived, for two years. They, too, had a little pride in their Stark experiences. They were proud that they had survived, proud that they knew something of that intriguing place, America, and proud that they knew some Americans.

"Yup," Tom Gadwah would say, "We all got along pretty good." And now the time had come to move along.

8

Commencement

Washington had a difficult time deciding when to ship the German prisoners of war back to Europe. With war's end, civilian issues reasserted themselves. The new Truman Administration would bow to political pressure on the issue of repatriation as soon as it could determine in which direction the pressure was being applied. At first a number of interest groups and politicians pushed for the immediate repatriation of all German prisoners of war. Their motives were emotional and economic. Bellicose congressmen would not hear of patriotic American fighting men returning to find enemy prisoners enjoying life on American soil. More important, American veterans should not have to compete with prisoners of war for employment.[1] Although it was unlikely that returning American servicemen would seek menial jobs performed by prisoner-of-war labor, the War Department took immediate steps to reassure labor leaders and politicians that the government was committed to rapid repatriation. No American would be denied a job by prisoner-of-war labor. Two months following the end of hostilities, in November 1945, the First Service Command informed the Brown Company that in the near future they could expect official termination of contract labor furnished to them through Camp Stark.[2]

However, soon after the government announced rapid repatriation in response to pressure applied about civilian unemployment, even greater pressure was applied to slow the repatriation process. From Germany the military government claimed it could not cope with any more mouths to feed in that devastated country. The occupation authorities also wished to avoid political problems created by the return of large groups of former prisoners of war, which included many Nazis.[3] In the United States, the agricultural interests and a growing number of politicians demanded that repatriation be halted so that prisoners of war could perform necessary agricultural labor. Some politicians from agricultural regions who had earlier called upon the War Department to ship the Germans to Europe immediately, reversed themselves, now demanding that they stay indefinitely in the United States as farm laborers. Farmers had planted or signed agricultural contracts under the assumption that prisoner-of-war labor would remain to do the harvesting. They protested vehemently against the government's plan to remove it in mid-season. In New Hampshire, the Brown Company demonstrated to the army that it would be impossible for it to find civilian labor sufficient to fulfill its existing contracts if it were to lose its prisoner-of-war labor.[4] Within two weeks, the army agreed to extend the prisoner-of-war labor program at Camp Stark until February 1946. As the February deadline drew near, President Truman bowed to political pressure and real agricultural needs, ordering a sixty-day extension of prisoner-of-war labor in pulpwood harvesting and other critical areas.[5] The contradictory indications confused and frustrated Camp Stark guards and prisoners alike. A sign that they might remain for a while, such as opening a new cutting area, would be followed by a sign that the Germans would be leaving soon, such as placing their pay in an account to be released in Germany.[6] A few of the prisoners of war had already left Stark. Soon after VE Day the Frenchman and two Dutchmen who had been taken into the Wehrmacht were transferred to Camp Houlton and then sent back to Europe.[7] Another group left in January 1946 to attend the six day re-education program at Fort Eustis, Virginia. From there they went directly to Germany with an offer of employment in the American military government.[8]

Not all the Germans wanted to go home. Some of the younger men at Camp Stark, having no established life or family in Germany waiting for them, would have preferred to remain in the United States. They had sensed the opportunities that American society offered and would have opted for life in the United States had they been permitted. Other men desired to remain in America not only because of the appeal of their new land but also because of their fears of returning to Soviet-occupied eastern Germany. A few men had no German home to which they could return; their regions of Germany had been annexed by Poland or the Soviet Union. These men asked the American authorities if they could remain. "Red," the cook, sobbed as he begged the captain to allow him somehow to stay.[9] But the War Department insisted that all prisoners of war be repatriated.

There were many German prisoners of war all across the United States whose acquired taste for American life made them want to remain. After they returned to Germany, most of them became involved with work and family there. Some, however, began the long process of applying for an immigrant visa. It is impossible to determine the number of former prisoners of war who eventually made their way back to the United States as immigrants. One knowledgeable estimate puts the figure at roughly 5 thousand (about the same as the number of Hessians who stayed behind after the Revolutionary War).[10] Five Camp Stark prisoners of war became American or Canadian citizens.

In May the Germans began to leave Stark. Many sought out their American friends—guards, foremen, civilians—to say farewell. The Americans made sure to say goodbye to a special prisoner or two. There were tears, and promises to write. The Germans would leave something of themselves behind and take something of the village with them. A group marched along the road to the station, the same road on which they had marched to the camp two years before. Back then a few Americans who looked out their windows had stared apprehensively. Now they stood in front of their houses and waved. Foreman Tom Gadwah lived next door to the Percy station. The column of men swung through his door yard, leaving as presents for him a pile of sweaters, woolen caps, and cigarettes. They shook his hand, hopped on the train, and were gone.[11]

German prisoner-of-war attitudes toward Americans underwent several dramatic changes during the prisoners' stay in the

United States. Initial Nazi-engendered stereotypes gave way in some cases to a tentative openness, a somewhat naive accommodation, and even friendship. Then came the spring of 1945, the concentration camp films, the end of the war, the harsh restrictions, rumors of delayed repatriation or even slave labor in Europe. All this placed great strain on the new German-American relations. In Stark the bonds held, in other places they broke. But in late 1945 and early 1946 attitudes began to change again, nourished positively by renewed American generosity and German optimism.[12] Then, as the Germans began to leave the United States, many with renewed admiration for America, one more bitter blow dashed German hopes and embittered the German prisoners of war against the Americans once again. About half of the returning Germans learned suddenly that they were not bound for home after all. A deal struck between the United States and its allies consigned German prisoners of war to indefinite terms in labor battalions working in war-damaged Britain or France.

The Germans from Camp Stark learned of their diversion to these labor projects after they left Stark, usually in Camp Houlton, although some were not informed until they were at sea on the way back to Europe. Even forty years later, their anger remained. They felt this policy was simply slave-trading, and that it was not only cruel but also foolish for the United States to pursue a policy that endangered or destroyed the favorable German attitude toward democracy and the United States which American authorities had attempted to implant in German prisoners of war.[13]

About half of the Germans from Camp Stark were forced to serve labor terms in Great Britain ranging from six to eighteen months. Their work on English and Welsh farms was not as difficult as wood cutting in New Hampshire, but the unexpected delay in returning home made the time pass unusually slowly. Their resentment of apparent American duplicity did not extend to the Americans they knew from Camp Stark or Stark village, who neither made the decision nor in most cases even knew about it. But it did slow down their growing appreciation of the significance of the Camp Stark experience. The official American involvement in the decision to assign Germans to the labor term eclipsed for a while the warm feelings toward America that Stark had kindled.

The American soldiers left Camp Stark, also, moving to old or new home towns across the country. A handful continued in the military. Captain Kobus, for example, served his next tour of duty in American-occupied Germany, where he and his wife adopted a 3-year-old German orphan girl. Some of the army guards stayed relatively close to Stark. The half dozen who married local girls settled down in Berlin, most securing jobs at the paper mill. One M.P. from Camp Stark stayed in police work, eventually becoming police chief in Berlin. The civilian foremen and the other people of Stark did not leave, of course, but Camp Stark had left them. It had brought some excitement to their town, but, like most of Stark's excitement, it passed. The people turned to mundane peacetime pursuits.

For a while, a few letters crossed the ocean. Lieutenant Roland Rief had an address book of Camp Stark names, American and German, and he wrote to them all. But he moved around and they moved around, and eventually he wrote only to a few Army buddies. Civilian foreman Winston Hart—the Germans called him "Hemlock" because of his rugged stature—kept in touch with his new friend Otto Triebel. When Triebel's English began to fade, he sent only blank picture postcards of his town, Eisenach, and its famed Wartburg. Then his son, Siegfried, became a pen-pal for several years of Hart's daughter Carolyn. Foreman Benny House and his wife Urania kept in touch with Austrian August Jurs for about a year. Jurs' life in postwar Graz was made easier by the cartons of cigarettes (for use as currency) and chocolate bars (for his children) sent by his friends in Stark. Dr. Foster heard once from his friend and former German medic, a letter revealing the broken spirit of postwar Germany:

> January 28, 1947
>
> Dear Sir:
>
> Too let you know I am home now after I have been 8 months in England. Home, et should not be called so but et is at least the land were I am born, all you find is Ruins, Wracks, Sick and Cripples, the rest do not want to do verry well. From my Wife and the Boy, I find no trace. Actually I am working in the american Eng.

Dept. at Hanau. There is absolutely no chance to work in the Hospital seem that there is not the materiel necessary to help everybody.

I hope Sir that you will let me know were the claims of the Medical Supply Depot at Portland after thy were throug with the Inventory of the Materiel we send down from the Dispensary. I dit not like the way the Materiel had to stay down there without Guard/? Please will you.

Now to let you know about my own situation, I am out of everything wich was my own, and am living with peoples I did never see befor, feed and tabacco are things you get wenn there are enough, so I have to run from one shop to the other to get the daily rations. If et is possible for you and not to mutch asked would you please be so kind and send a Paket with food and some Tabacco? Thys only, if et is possible.

Wishing everybody is well at your home, and in good health

I remain yours
Johann Jarclovski

Jarclovski never wrote again.

When the letters stopped, the Germans and Americans of Camp Stark lost touch with each other. Silence separated them for nearly forty years. But memories of each other stayed alive. The Americans all remembered "Red"—his good food, his German rendition of "Don't Fence Me In." When former guards would meet on a Berlin street they might laugh as they talked of Tatzko, the "gypsy," and his Sunday afternoon acrobatic and juggling performance. Warren Hoyt liked to show people the snapshot of himself, the American army guard, sitting contentedly while the prisoner of war, Tatzko, stood behind him, axe in hand. He also liked to show the little matchbox house the prisoners made for his birthday, and the nightstand they gave to his wife. Warren thought of the Germans often and wished he had not forgotten their names. His buddy Carl would joke about the Austrian girl promised to him in marriage by her brother, a prisoner of war. Her picture looked very pretty, he would say. They all remembered the one they called "the Duke." He was fastidious, his clothes always clean and pressed, his moustache twirled. He would change to his dirty work clothes only when they arrived in the woods, and then change back to clean clothes for the return truck ride to camp. They also remembered young Clauss, "who spoke English real good." The American veterans of Camp Stark swapped stories about how clever the Germans were with their hands. Bald-headed Hans, the tinsmith, could make anything out of metal and never needed a pattern. When the boss foreman wrecked his car, Hans fixed it on his own time. They said you would never know where dents had been. When General Eisenhower made his distinctive jacket popular, the German tailor converted the Camp Stark guards' regular army jackets into Eisenhower jackets.

Urania House, a schoolteacher, talked with more of the prisoners of war than any other woman in Stark. She remembered one little 17-year-old, whom she told about Devil's Slide and Devil's Hopyard, a local cliff and a local ravine, and taught to spell Indian words like Ammonoosuc. Most of all, Urania remembered August and the flowers. She liked to tell the story about how she went to Emerson's store in Groteton and said she wanted some seeds for the German prisoners. The man in the store gave her a bag, perhaps over five dollars worth, and said not to tell anyone he gave so much. "August," she said, "was so surprised! He'd leave flowers for me when I stopped at the camp on the way home from the schoolhouse."[14]

August made a model boat. It ended up in a glass case in the Stark school so all the children could see it and remember the Germans. But then somehow the case was broken, someone took it away to be repaired, and the boat never came back. The older people were saddened to see an important link between the town and the Germans disappear. New school children felt they missed out on something.

Meanwhile Camp Stark began to disappear. The buildings were dismantled, the lumber auctioned off. Most of Camp Stark ended up in the hands of Chubby Willette who used the wood to build the C&S Bowladrome in Berlin. It burned down. A few boards from the camp became the awning on the Stark General Store. Some local people kept scraps of lumber as souvenirs of Camp Stark. The grass and bushes grew up, and the surrounding forest began to reclaim the site of Camp Stark. The people had put Camp Stark behind them. But remembrance kept it from staying there.

9

Auf Wiedersehen

September 1986. A small group of Germans, former prisoners of
war and their wives, their eyes ringed with fatigue after a long
trans-Atlantic flight, squinted in the bright sun at the Boston
airport. "So," one of them chuckled. "We've come again to
America!" Then he said quietly, soberly, "It is for peace." *"Ja,"*
nodded the others, *"Es ist für Frieden."*

Although the narrowest conclusions about Camp Stark can
be drawn in terms of the War Department's objectives for the
prisoner-of-war program in general and the need for prisoner-
of-war labor in particular, Camp Stark did more for people and
peace than for pulpwood. In the immediate postwar climate,
self-congratulation was the order of the day. Although the
Provost Marshal General's office had been initially unen-
thusiastic about its responsibilities for prisoners of war, it
praised its own performance, concluding that the prisoner-of-
war labor program had offset the wartime labor shortage and
even made a profit.[1] The Brown Company credited Camp
Stark with producing approximately 45,000 cords of pulpwood, much of it cut on steep and difficult terrain. The prisoners of war supplied more than 13 percent of the Brown
Company's total pulpwood requirements, enabling the company to meet its wartime production schedule.[2] Captain Kobus
received a commendation medal for the camp's pulpwood production and its profit of more than 1 million dollars.[3] Of course,
claims of profit were based upon the assumption that the government was obliged to maintain its prisoners of war, although
even the most efficient use of prisoner-of-war laborers did not

cover the basic cost of their maintenance.[4]

The story of German prisoners of war in the United States is a strange weave of threads of war and peace. The U.S. Government treated its German captives well; they fared better than their wives and children, many of whom died in American air raids. Many German prisoners of war in the United States lived under conditions that permitted them to enjoy peacetime comforts. A primary rationale for America's benevolent and peaceful treatment of its German prisoners was to aid prosecution of the war against the Nazi regime by coaxing German soldiers to surrender. The reason for the war, as far as most Americans were concerned, was to restore peace. And peace meant not only the cessation of hostilities but also the replacement of Nazi tyranny by a peaceful and democratic Germany. In many ways Camp Stark anticipated this. Its men and women, Americans and Germans alike, became war heroes by becoming peace heroes, reaching out to each other in decency across barriers of nationality and war. But for some of them it took forty years to realize what they had done.

After the war, as people resumed their lives, the memory of Camp Stark lingered, although its significance remained blurred. As the years went by, oldtimers in the village remained proud to remember the camp, while the younger people became intrigued with the tales they heard. As the former prisoners of war built new lives in a new Germany, they paused from time to time to reflect upon their American days. Each side began to come to terms with all it had meant.

Twice in the 1970s, as postwar international tourism became commonplace, Stark was visited by former prisoners of war who had since emigrated to Canada. One merely drove through, speaking only with a storekeeper in nearby Groveton who knew little about the camp. The other spent a few hours at the tiny Stark general store, talking with one of the former Brown Company foremen. He had to move on quickly, but his visit served to sharpen recollections of the camp.[5] That October afternoon in 1982, when I showed up, the first of many American Camp Stark veterans said, "Wouldn't it be something if a bunch of those German boys would come back here!" Later, in Germany, I discovered an equally strong desire on the part of the German veterans to return to the rugged hills and gentle people of northern New Hampshire.

The time had come for the people of Camp Stark to make something of it. The intervening years had been good for most of them, better than the war years that had first brought them together and then receded into history while a new generation and even another has been born. Today, the grandparents have something important to say to the children and grandchildren. The present reshapes the past, and the people of Camp Stark wanted their past—the war, the camp, all their pain and sadness—to serve the interests of their present world as it clung to a fragile peace.

Originally, when the idea of a reunion was broached, a dozen former prisoners of war planned to return to Stark, but infirmities cut their number to the five who arrived in New Hampshire with families and friends in late September 1986. I took them first to Colby-Sawyer College in New London, New Hampshire, where they spoke to my students, strolled through the hill-top town, and excitedly took snapshots of a stray moose that wandered onto the campus shortly after their arrival. Meanwhile, a hundred miles north, Stark village prepared for the biggest day in its history. Madeleine Croteau assumed command. Vivacious and energetic, Madeleine had grown up with stories of Camp Stark told by her mother-in-law, Urania House, the local schoolteacher who had befriended several of the Germans. A few years before, when Madeleine visited her daughter and son-in-law, who were stationed in Germany, she had half-hoped to encounter a German from Camp Stark. Now, instead, they were coming to her village. Madeleine was a resourceful woman who knew how to make the little village get things done. The people of Stark pitched in with fresh white paint, a new rope for the church bell, freshly harvested orange pumpkins stacked around the town sign, yards of colorful bunting draped along the bridge, two new hooks for the German flag on the school house flagpole, and a big banner on the town hall announcing the approaching German-American Friendship Day.

Those who had prayed all that rainy summer for a good day smiled to see the September Saturday dawn bright and clear. The caravan of cars and vans left Colby-Sawyer College, wound its way through the White Mountains, and two hours later rounded the bend of the Upper Ammonoosuc River below the steep, colorful slope of Mill Mountain, to enter Stark. In each car, jovial banter gave way to hushed stillness as the returning Germans coped with the range of emotions evoked by their return to the now festive village where they had been prisoners of war forty years earlier.

The initial meeting of the German and American veterans of Camp Stark was planned for the more private setting on the far side of the bridge. There, Albert Lang and Hermann Uelsmann recognized each other immediately. The American had less hair, the German more—in the form of the grey beard he now sported. The other former guards, foremen, and prisoners mingled quickly, patting each other's paunches, tousling thinning hair, hovering over yellowed snapshots. Outside the tight circle, German and American family members beamed.

One of the former American guards, Bob Simonian, had been unsure about returning. The war had been hard on him. After having been pinned down for weeks in combat against the Germans at Anzio, he had been evacuated to the United States on a hospital ship, and then had been assigned to guard duty at Camp Stark. After a while at Stark, Simonian was transferred to a prisoner-of-war camp in northern Maine. There combat stress finally caught up with him. One day in a watchtower he felt himself becoming confused, turning the machine gun on the Germans below, about to squeeze the trigger. At the last moment he caught himself, asked to be relieved, and spent the next months and years in and out of army hospitals, attempting to cope with his anger and fear. He hesitated to attend the German-American reunion in Stark. "Go ahead," his wife Doris said, "It'll be good for you. You'll see they're just like you, a bunch of old men, proud of their children." Simonian decided to go, and, healed, found it was easy to fit right in.

At one o'clock, the tolling church bell, a musket volley, and skirling bagpipes announced the start of the festivities. The reunited Germans and Americans marched together along the smooth planks of the covered bridge into the sunlight on the front side, amazed to see the thousand people who had come to Stark that day to welcome them back. Journalists, wireservice photographers, and network television crews hovered around. They would carry the Camp Stark story to the rest of the nation. Words of greeting from the selectmen calmed the excited crowd. The school children who attended the two-room Stark school were dressed up in colorful vests. They warbled songs in German and English. Both nations' flags were run up the flagpole, and as the two national anthems echoed off the cliffs, a number of the honored guests' eyes welled with tears. Gerhard Clauss was astounded by the stirring welcome. Standing along the fence near the covered bridge, Klaus Wiemann joked with his former guards, while his wife and daughter smiled proudly. "Usually I don't care much for speeches," one of the former American soldiers said afterwards, "but those speeches up at the tent were the best part of the whole day."

After the welcoming ceremony, the group boarded yellow school buses for the short ride to the site of Camp Stark, now little more than an overgrown clearing in the roadside forest. Two hundred chairs under the striped tent filled rapidly, while other visitors crowded around the sides. The Camp Stark veterans and their families sat expectantly in the front rows awaiting the serious part of the program. The speakers addressed not only the history of Camp Stark, but also the burden of a larger history. Although the mood was festive, this was, after all, an unusual reunion, commemorating a prison camp. Life in Camp Stark often had been unpleasant, marked by anxiety, tension, strife, and despair. Those had been dark years and days of sadness in Germany and America. But these people looked back to moments of light, gestures of kindness, attempts to understand. My colleague from Dartmouth College, German-American historian Hans Michael Ermarth, spoke in English and German of the continuing role of the Camp Stark experience in fostering understanding or

> *Verstehen,* as the Germans call it. They quite rightly have their own word for it—and a special word at that—because they have a whole tradition concerning this matter. Perhaps owing to their position in Europe and their own historical development—looking across many boundaries and looking across many ages in the past, perhaps also owing to the feeling of being misunderstood—whatever the reasons, there is a long German legacy on the question of

understanding others and on the conditions which understanding requires if it is to endure.

Such human understanding of things human is very basic and simple, but also very complicated and delicate. Understanding is what links us to others, enables us to function, to communicate and participate, and to carry on our lives. We have to rely upon it all the time, and yet it is fragile and often unnoticeably disrupted, with serious and even grave consequences—as wars testify with terrible regularity. Understanding is required to grasp what it was like to be in a prisoner-of-war camp or in a concentration camp during World War II; it is required to grasp what it was like to live in Hitler's Germany, to lose a total war, or to be a citizen of a country like the United States, which invites uneasiness or resentment in the world because of its enormous power—or, likewise, to be a citizen of a country like West Germany which invites uneasiness because of its past.

But there is a dilemma here. For if understanding is tied closely to actual experiences and the sharing of experiences, then the passing of the generation of participants and the fading of experiences—even if they were difficult and traumatic—means the inevitable loss of a crucial dimension of understanding. There is in fact much talk now about a "gap" of understanding, of ignorance, and even indifference. The sheer passage of time may be producing a historical bottom-line or *Schlussstrich,* which blocks mutual understanding.

This gathering can restore some degree of personal immediacy and lived experience for the participants—but even more importantly it can go beyond that to impart historical meaning and create understanding among those who did not go through those events in the past. Somewhat in the spirit of the famous New England Town Meeting, our latter-day gathering at Camp Stark—a very peculiar kind of reunion—can signify mutual understanding at a grassroots, person-to-person level. It is not monumental and grandiose, but it is filled with human meaning of a concrete sort.

The Boston Consulate General of the Federal Republic of Germany was represented by Hartmut Lang, whose remarks were also directed to the challenge of discharging the burden of history without dismissing it. The attentive audience held its breath when Lang's voice broke with emotion as he spoke softly in barely accented English.

To be a prisoner of war isn't easy. But it's much more difficult to be the guards of prisoners of war. The guard knows that he must mis-

trust the prisoner, but the guard also knows that he has responsibilities towards his prisoner. It must be difficult to strike a balance
between these sometimes conflicting duties.

In the case of the United States, it was well known among German soldiers in the last war on which side the scales of that balance
would come down: on the side of decency to the defeated adversary.
To a German soldier then, being taken prisoner by U.S. troops
amounted to winning a ticket to peace and fair treatment.

The experiences of those former German prisoners of war are
not forgotten. I'm sure they have contributed substantially to the
image the average German has of the average American. It is the
image of the fair and quietly decent American. This image, I
assure you, is alive in Germany.

After dedicating an official roadside historical marker, the
Camp Stark veterans, along with their attending flock of new
friends, reporters, photographers, and television crews made
their way back to the German-American fair by then in full
swing in the town center: exhibits of prisoner-of-war painting
and handicrafts, New Hampshire craft vendors, knockwurst
and cotton candy, German-American Friendship Day shirts
and caps, a brass band playing German songs. Relaxed now,
the Germans and Americans talked among themselves and to
inquiring strangers about what it all meant. They laughed
about the bear cub, grimaced about the insects, shivered as they
remembered the cold. But there was also more somber talk of
hard work, the hated quota, separation from loved ones, squabbles among the prisoners of war, the harsh conditions suffered
after the German surrender, and the fear they had felt of the
unknown future. Gerhard Clauss compared it to driving
through a long tunnel with no glimpse of light in the end. Now,
looking back, it seemed less troublesome and more meaningful.
Americans and Germans sympathized with each other, all having been tossed around the globe by a terrible war. They now
realized clearly what years ago they only dimly perceived. They
had done something special. In a difficult situation, they indeed
had made Camp Stark an island of decency in a world at war.

As the sun finally sunk behind the northern ridge of Pilot
Mountain, and cool shadows filled the narrow valley, the Camp
Stark family sat down to dinner. For the first time ever, the long
tables in the rustic town hall were draped with linen, set with

fancy dishes, decorated with harvest flowers and tiny German and American flags. A moment of silence after grace allowed reflection on the unique gathering. Then the caterers burst from the kitchen with a holiday turkey dinner with all the trimmings. Hans Richter and Albert Petermann looked around the room, overwhelmed by the celebration. Former guard Warren Hoyt's rugged face creased into a grin as he spoke of the "beautiful feeling I've got tonight, I'm so happy about it, from the bottom of my heart." The congenial crowd shared toasts, jokes, gifts, and popular songs—the lyrics in two languages. After the meal, Madeleine Croteau stood up and tried to put into a few words the significance of Camp Stark—past, present, and future—to her little village. She spoke of the elderly man who had stopped at her house earlier in the week as the people of Stark prepared for their big day

> In our conversation, he looked at me and said, "Lady, I want you to know it's a great thing you are doing here!" I looked at him in surprise and asked him, "What do you mean?" He said, "Lady, more towns should be doing things like this. You should be proud." His eyes filled with tears as he continued, "You are fostering love; you are fostering peace; you are fostering friendship; and most important, you are fostering forgiveness."
>
> I hope that on this 27th day of September, 1986, in Stark, New Hampshire, population 489, we have fostered love; we have fostered peace; we have fostered friendship; and most of all, we have fostered forgiveness.

Then, spontaneously, everyone linked arms and sang "Don't Fence Me In" and "Auld Lang Syne," prolonging an evening never envisioned forty years before. The visiting Germans spent the night in homes in the village, congregating the next morning for a memorial church service alternating in German and English. Past noon, they wanted, once more, to go back to the camp site, this time with no crowds, no brass band, no television crews. Each man walked slowly in the small clearing, silent in his own thoughts. I watched them, and thought of the responses they had made a year before in Germany when I had shown them a photograph of Camp Stark today, the buildings gone, their place taken by flowers and trees. Each man had stared in surprise at the picture, thought for a moment, and said quietly, *"Es ist besser so."* Fall flowers waved in a warm breeze, a few yellow birch leaves floated down, a chickadee chirped in a lacy larch tree. *Es ist besser so.*

It was time to leave. The Germans at Camp Stark said their farewells and drove away. Madeleine stood by the new historical marker, waved, and called, *"Auf Wiedersehen!"* They'll be back, she thought. So will their children.

Notes

1. Introduction
(pp. 1–6)

1. Gerald H. Davis, "Prisoners of War in Twentieth Century War Economies," *Journal of Contemporary History,* Oct. 1977, p. 624.

2. Arnold Krammer, *Nazi Prisoners of War in America,* (Briarcliff Manor, N.Y.: Stein and Day, 1979), pp. 271–272; George G. Lewis and John Mewha, *History of Prisoner of War Utilization by the United States Army, 1776–1945,* (Washington: Department of the Army, 1955), Pamphlet No. 20–213, pp. 90, 91. Among the "German" prisoners of war in the United States and in Camp Stark were many Austrian soldiers. This book, like U.S. official documents, includes Austrian captives when referring to German prisoners of war.

3. W. Stanley Hoole, "Alabama's World War II Prisoner of War Camps," *Alabama Review,* vol. 20, Jan. 1967, pp. 112, 113; George T. Mazuzan and Nancy Walker, "Restricted Areas: German Prisoner of War Camps in Western New York, 1944–1946," *New York History,* 59, Jan. 1978, p. 72.

2. A Place Called Stark
(pp. 7–15)

1. Stark Bicentennial Committee, *History of Stark,* (Littleton, N.H.: Courier Printing Co.: 1974), pp. 139, 140.

2. Interview, Urania House, Franklin, N.H., Oct. 8, 1982.

3. *History of Stark,* pp. 11, 118, 146.

4. *Boston* (Mass.) *Sunday Globe,* Mar. 3, 1985, pp. 1, 78.

5. Interview, Alban Keenan, Portsmouth, N.H., Apr. 10, 1983.

6. Interview, House, Oct. 8, 1982.

7. *History of Stark,* pp. 191–193.

8. Letter (interoffice), J. H. Merrill to P. W. Churchill, Brown Co., Berlin, N.H., Jan. 12, 1944.

9. *Berlin* (N.H.) *Reporter,* Feb. 17, 1944, p. 2; *Manchester* (N.H.) *Union,* Mar. 2, 1944, p. 1.

10. Interviews: Carl Giordono, Berlin, N.H., June 29, 1983; Warren Hoyt, Berlin, N.H., Jan. 18, 1983.

11. Interviews: Elizabeth Foster, Keene, N.H., Feb. 27, 1983; Gertrude Kobus, Peachtree City, Ga., July 2, 1987.

12. Interview, Alexandium Kobus, Peachtree City, Ga., July 2, 1987.

13. Interviews: Winnefred Hart, Pennacook, N.H., Oct. 20, 1982; A. Kobus.

14. Interview, House, Oct. 8, 1982.
15. Interviews: House, June 7, 1983; E. L., July 14, 1983.
16. Interviews: E. L., House, Oct. 8, 1982; Giordono, Sept. 13, 1983; Hans Wenzel, New London, N.H., May 14, 1987.

3. Americans and Prisoners of World War II
(pp. 16–27)

1. Lewis and Mewha, p. 18–21; Ralph Busco and Douglas Adler, "German and Italian Prisoners of War in Utah and Idaho," *Utah Historical Quarterly*, vol. 39, 1971, p. 56.
2. Busco and Adler, p. 56; Krammer, p. 37; Herston Cooper, *Crossville: How Did We Treat POW's?* (Art Circle Public Library, Crossville, Tenn., n.d.), p. 3.
3. Judith Gansberg, *Stalag: U.S.A.* (New York: Thomas Crowell Co., 1977), p. 3; Krammer, p. 38; Lewis and Mewha, p. 66; Mazuzan and Walker, p. 56.
4. Krammer, p. viii; Gansberg, p. 4.
5. Gansberg, p. 5.
6. Allan Bosworth, *America's Concentration Camps,* (New York: W. W. Norton and Co., 1967), pp. 46, 47.
7. Krammer, pp. 2, 3, 43.
8. Walter Lunden, "Captivity Psychosis Among Prisoners of War," *Journal of Criminal Law and Criminology,*" vol. 39, 1949, p. 725.
9. Reinhold Pabel, *Enemies Are Human,* (Philadelphia: John Winston Co., 1955), p. 149; Edward Shils and Morris Janowitz, "Cohesion and Disintegration in the Wehrmacht in World War II," *Public Opinion Quarterly,* Summer 1948, vol. 12, no. 2, pp. 280, 291.
10. Lunden, pp. 727, 728.
11. Interviews: Hermann Osmer, Harpstedt, Germany, July 10, 1985; E. L.
12. Interview, Osmer; Krammer, p. 17.
13. Kurt Böhme and Helmut Wolf, *Aufzeichnungen über die Kriegsgefangenschaft im Westen; Geschichte der Deutschen Kriegsgefangenen des Zweiten Weltkrieges,* (Munich, 1973), pp. 94, 95; Yvonne Humphrey, "On Shipboard with German Prisoners," *American Journal of Nursing,* vol. 43, no. 9, Sept. 1943, pp. 821, 822.
14. Interview, Gerhard Clauss, Lippstadt, Germany, July 11, 1985.
15. Böhme, p. 97; Hoole, p. 87; Krammer, p. 16.
16. Pabel, p. 148; Krammer, p. 16.
17. Pabel, pp. 137, 138.
18. Shils and Janowitz, p. 298.
19. Interview, E. L.; Krammer, p. 6.
20. Pabel, p. 148; Krammer, p. 19; interviews: Clauss, E. L.
21. Robert Tissing, "Stalag-Texas," *Military History of Texas and the Southwest,* vol. 13, Fall 1986, p. 24; Krammer, p. 26.
22. Krammer, pp. 35, 272.
23. Ibid., p. 27; Cooper, pp. 36, 37.
24. Krammer, pp. 153, 154; Edward Pluth, "Prisoners of War Employed in Minnesota During World War II," *Minnesota History,* Winter 1975, p. 299.
25. Shils and Janowitz, p. 312.

26. *Newsweek,* May 7, 1945, pp. 58–61; Gansberg, p. 39.

27. *Newsweek,* Apr. 16, 1945; American National Red Cross, *Prisoner of War Bulletin,* vol. 3, no. 6, June 1945.

28. John Vietor, *Time Out: American Airmen at Stalag Luft I,* (New York: Richard R. Smith Publisher, Inc., 1951), pp. 86, 87.

29. Gansberg, p. 38.

30. Krammer, p. 78; Beverly Smith, "The Afrika Korps Comes to America," *American Magazine,* vol. 136, Aug. 1943, p. 28; John Hammond Moore, "Italian POWs in America: War Is Not Always Hell," *Prologue,* Fall 1976, pp. 141, 147.

31. Robert Devoe, "Our 'Pampered' War Prisoners," *Colliers,* Oct. 14, 1944, p. 58; Krammer, p. 45.

32. Smith, p. 83; Devoe, p. 57.

33. *Newsweek,* May 7, 1945, p. 58.

34. Interviews: Linwood Gadwah, Stark, N.H., Oct. 9, 1982; House, A. Kobus.

35. Davis, p. 629.

36. Lewis and Mawha, p. 57.

37. Krammer, pp. 80, 81; Lewis and Mewha, p. 89.

38. Jack Spidle, "Axis Invasion of the American West; POW's in New Mexico," *New Mexico Historical Review,* vol. 99, no. 2, Apr. 1974, p. 109.

39. Lewis and Mewha, p. 106.

40. Krammer, p. 87.

41. Pluth, p. 295.

42. Krammer, pp. 105, 106.

43. Merrill Pritchett and William Shea, "The Afrika Korps in Arkansas, 1943–1946," *Arkansas Historical Quarterly,* vol. 37, no. 1, Spring 1978, p. 18; Lewis and Mewha, p. 132.

44. *Littleton* (N.H.) *Courier,* Aug. 8, 1943, p. 1.

45. Letter, F. W. Hunter, War Manpower Commission, to H. G. Schanche, Brown Co., Aug. 5, 1943.

4. The Germans
(pp. 28–39)

1. Krammer, pp. 13, 14.

2. "German POW Camps in Maine," *Maine Sunday Telegram,* Portland, Me., Aug. 12, 1984, p. 44a; interview, Henry Ehrmann, Hanover, N.H., June 11, 1983; Krammer, p. 165.

3. Henry Faulk, *Group Captives, The Re-education of German Prisoners of War in Britain, 1945–1948,* (London: Chatto and Windus, 1977), p. 27; Heinz Ansbacher, "Attitudes of German Prisoners of War: A Study in the Dynamics of National-Socialistic Followership," *Psychological Monographs,* vol. 62, no. 1, 1948, p. 10.

4. Ansbacher, p. 16.

5. Ibid., pp. 24, 32; Faulk, p. 22.

6. Ansbacher, p. 33; Faulk, p. 23.

7. Faulk, p. 19; Edward Shils and Morris Janowitz, "Cohesion and Disin-

tegration in the Wehrmacht in World War II," *Public Opinion Quarterly*, Summer 1948, vol. 2, no. 2, pp. 280–315.

8. Faulk, p. 24; Ansbacher, p. 22.

9. David Levy, "The German Anti-Nazi: A Case Study," *American Journal of Orthopsychiatry*, no. 16, July 1946, pp. 508, 509, 515.

10. Krammer, p. 149.

11. Ibid., p. 161.

12. Interviews: Ehrmann, A. Kobus; Krammer, p. 161.

13. Shils and Janowitz, p. 291; interview, Ehrmann.

14. Lewis and Mewha, p. 161.

15. Gansberg, pp. 52, 53; Krammer, pp. 169, 170.

16. John Mason Brown, "German Prisoners of War in the United States," *The American Journal of International Law*, vol. 39, 1945, p. 213; Daniel Costelle, *Les Prisonniers*, (Paris: Flammarion, 1975), pp. 64, 65; Krammer, p. 173.

17. Vicki Baum, "Land of the Free," *Colliers*, Aug. 19, 1944, pp. 11, 12, 40–42; interview, Ehrmann.

18. Krammer, pp. 174, 175; Costelle, pp. 71, 72.

19. Gansberg, p. 62; interview, Ehrmann.

20. Manfred Hornung, *PW*, (Vienna: Verlag, 1959), pp. 144, 145; Terry Paul Wilson, "The Afrika Korps in Oklahoma: Fort Reno's Prisoner of War Compound," *The Chronicles of Oklahoma*, vol. 52, no. 3, Fall 1974, p. 366.

21. Charles Burdick, "Prisoners as Soldiers, The German 999th Penal Division," *The Army Quarterly and Defense Journal*, 102, Oct. 1971–July 1972, pp. 65, 66.

22. Burdick, p. 66.

23. Gansberg, p. 58.

24. Interview, Clauss; Paul Carrell, tr. Mervyn Savill, *The Foxes of the Desert*, (New York: E. P. Dutton and Co., 1961), p. 348; James Lucas, *Panzer Army Afrika*, (San Rafael: Presidio Press, 1978), p. 84.

25. Interview, E. L.; German-American Emergency Conference, *The German American*, vol. 3, no. 2, May 15, 1944, p. 1.

26. Burdick, p. 67.

27. Interview, E. L.; Burdick, pp. 6, 68.

28. Albert Seaton, *The German Army*, (New York: St. Martin's Press, 1982), pp. 197, 198; Carrell, p. 348; Modern Military Headquarters Branch, National Archives, Washington, D.C., Guide No. 76, 999 Afrika-Division, Unit History.

29. Burdick, p. 67.

30. Interview, Clauss.

31. Lucas, p. 184; Carrell, p. 348; Shils and Janowitz, pp. 280, 284.

32. Interview, E. L.

33. Burdick, p. 69; interview, E. L.

34. John Hammond Moore, "Hitler's Afrika Korps in New England," *Yankee*, June 1976, p. 83.

35. Interview, E. L.; letter, Eugen Kiefer to author, July 5, 1987; letter, Klaus Wiemann to author, June 29, 1985.

36. Interviews: Wenzel, E. L.

37. Interviews: August Jurs, Graz, Austria, July 15, 1984; A. N., Stuttgart, Germany, July 2, 1984; prisoner-of-war letter, Heinrich Wrede to J. Wrede, July 15, 1944.

38. M. Peter, International Red Cross, Camp Stark facilities report, visit, July 24, 1944, National Archives RG 389, PMGO, Box 2660.

39. Interview, Osmer.

40. Interview and diary, E. L.

41. Diary, E. L.

5. Strife in a Bitter Place
(pp. 40–75)

1. Hermann Jung, *Die deutschen Kriegsgefangenen in amerikanischer Hand,* Erich Maschke, ed. *Zur Geschichte der deutschen Kriegsgenfangenen des Zweiten Weltkrieges,* (Bielefeld: Verlag Gieseking, 1972), p. 178.

2. Interview, Klaus Wiemann, Malente, Germany, July 10, 1985; interview, A. Kobus.

3. Interviews: Clauss; Georges Zéler, Petite Rosselle, France, July 12, 1985.

4. Interviews: Clauss; A. Kobus; letter, Lt. Col. A. J. Lamoureaux, U.S. Army First Service Command, to P. W. Churchill, Brown Co., Aug. 2, 1944; Brown Co., L. Gagnon, Berlin, N.H.

5. Interview, A. Kobus; letter, Lt. Col. William Bingham, U.S. Army First Service Command, to Herman Schanche, Brown Co., May 27, 1944.

6. Interviews: Glenn Lunn, Stark, N.H., Aug. 4, 1983; A. Kobus.

7. Jake Spidle, "Invasion of the American West: POW's in New Mexico," *New Mexico Historical Review,* xlix, no. 2, Apr. 1974, p. 99.

8. Ralph A. Busco and Douglas D. Adler, "German and Italian Prisoners of War in Utah and Idaho," *Utah Historical Quarterly,* vol. 39, 1971, p. 67.

9. Interviews: Warren Hoyt, Berlin, N.H., Jan. 18, 1983; Carl Giordono, Berlin, N.H., Oct. 24, 1986; Vincent Caggiula, Colebrook, N.H., Aug. 5, 1983.

10. Interviews: Frank Chappell, Berlin, N.H., Sept. 13, 1983; Giordono.

11. Interviews: Linwood Gadwah, Stark, N.H., Oct. 9, 1982; House.

12. Jung, pp. 194, 195; interview, E. L.

13. Interviews: Wenzel, Clauss.

14. Interview and diary, E. L.

15. Interview, Hoyt; interview and diary, E. L.

16. Interviews: Albert Lang, West Milan, N.H., Aug. 16, 1983; Caggiula.

17. Philip Guyol, *Democracy Fights: A History of New Hampshire in World War II,* (Hanover, N.H., Dartmouth Publications, 1951), p. 44.

18. Letter, Bingham to P. W. Churchill, September 16, 1944.

19. Interview, A. Kobus.

20. Interview and diary, E. L.

21. Letter, Bingham to the Provost Marshal General, Dec. 14, 1944, National Archives RG 389, PMGO Box 2661.

22. Interview, E. L.

23. Interview, Albert Lang.

24. Interview, Giordono, Oct. 24, 1986.

25. J. Edgar Hoover, "Enemies at Large," *The American Magazine,* Apr. 1944, pp. 17, 97–100.

26. Krammer, p. 115.

27. Ibid., p. 115, 116.

28. Interview, A. Kobus; Robert Jackson, *A Taste of Freedom,* (London: Arthur Barker Ltd., 1964), p. 7.

29. Krammer, p. 126.

30. Ibid., p. 117.

31. John Hammond Moore, *The Faustball Tunnel,* (New York: Random House, 1978).

32. Reinhold Pabel, *Enemies Are Human,* (Philadelphia: J. Winston Co., 1955), p. 164.

33. "Hitler's Last Soldier in America Gives Up," *Newsweek,* Sept. 23, 1985, p. 33.

34. Interview, Giordono, Oct. 24, 1986.

35. Interview and diary, E. L.

36. Letter, Lamoureaux, First Service Command, to the Provost Marshal General, Aug. 1944,, National Archives, RG 389, PMGO, Box 1256.

37. Krammer, pp. 140–142.

38. Interviews: A. Kobus, Wiemann.

39. Interviews: A. Kobus, Clauss, Wiemann.

40. Interview, A. Kobus.

41. Interview, Giordono, June 29, 1983.

42. Interviews: Lunn, House; interview and diary, E. L.

43. Interview, Theodore Tausig, New Haven, Conn., Feb. 1, 1984.

44. *Berlin Reporter,* July 6, 1944, pp. 1, 3.

45. *Berlin Reporter,* Aug. 17, 1944, p. 1; interview, House.

46. Interview, House.

47. Interview, Hoyt.

48. Idem.

49. *Littleton Courier,* Aug. 24, 1944, p. 1.

50. Interview, House.

51. Interview, Giordono, June 29, 1983.

52. Letter, Lamoureaux to the Provost Marshal General, Sept. 4, 1944, National Archives, RG 389, PMGO, Box 256; *Littleton Courier,* Aug. 31, 1944, p. 1.

53. Interview, House.

54. *Berlin Reporter,* Oct. 19, 1944, pp. 1, 3; interview, Giordono, June 29, 1983; interview, Lang; interview and diary, E. L.

55. "Report on Construction and Discovery of Tunnel at Prisoner of War Branch Camp Stark, New Hampshire," National Archives, RG 389, PMGO, Enemy Information Bureau, Reporting Branch, Subject File, 1942–46, Entry 461, Box 2598; interviews: A. Kobus, Giordono, Chappell.

56. Interview, Tausig.

57. *New York Times,* Oct. 15, 1944, p. 11; *Berlin Reporter,* October 18, 1944, p. 1; interviews: A. Kobus, Chappell.

58. Interview, E. L.

59. Interview, Tausig.
60. Idem.
61. Interview and diary, E. L.; interview, Clauss.
62. Labor Reports, Camp Stark, National Archives, RG 389, PMGO, Box 2514; interview, A. Kobus.
63. Interview, A. Kobus.
64. Interviews: A. Kobus, Chappell.
65. Interviews: A. Kobus, Giordono.
66. Tape received from A. Kobus, Dec. 1983; interview, A. Kobus.
67. Interviews: A. Kobus, Foster.
68. Interviews: A. Kobus, Clauss.
69. Tape received from A. Kobus.
70. Interview, A. Kobus.
71. Krammer, p. 39; interview, A. Kobus.
72. Interview, Giordono.
73. Interview, A. Kobus.
74. Interview, A. Kobus; letter, Gen. Sherman Miles to P. W. Churchill, Brown Co., Sept. 13, 1944.
75. Walter A. Lunden, "Captivity Psychosis Among Prisoners of War," *Journal of Criminal Law and Criminology*, 39 (1949), p. 723.
76. Interviews: Willi Volz, Birmingham, England, July 26, 1985; Clauss, Wenzel, Giordono, Hoyt, Wiemann.
77. Jung, p. 7.
78. Spidle, p. 97; interviews: Wenzel, Zéler, Volz.
79. Interview and diary, E. L.; interview, Chappell.
80. Letter, E. L. to author, Oct. 1984.
81. Maj. F. L. Brown, Report to First Service Command, Apr. 2, 1945.
82. Interviews: Clauss, Wiemann, Wenzel, Chappell, Tausig.
83. Interviews: Clauss, Chappell.
84. Interview, Foster.
85. *The German-American*, vol. 3, no. 2, May 15, 1944, German-American Emergency Conference; interview and diary, E. L.
86. Interview, Wenzel.
87. Interview and diary, E. L.; interviews: Clauss, Wenzel, Volz, A. Kobus, Chappell.
88. Interview, Donald Beattie, Lyndonville, Vt., July 24, 1986.
89. Interview, A. Kobus.
90. Interviews: Zéler, Wenzel; interview and diary, E. L.

6. From Barriers to Bonds
(pp. 76–96)

1. Interview, Lang.
2. Interview, Wiemann.
3. Letter, Eugen Kiefer; interview, Gadwah.
4. Mt. Washington Observatory, *News Bulletin*, Aug. 1946; *Appalachia*, vol. 12,

no. 7, June 1946, p. 98; interview, Hans Richter, Idstein, Germany, July 12, 1985.

5. Interview, Giordono.

6. Interviews: Vincent Caggiula, Colebrook, N.H., Aug. 5, 1987; Chappell.

7. Krammer, p. 149; Spidle, p. 101.

8. Interviews: Allan Gurney, Laconia, N.H., July 16, 1986; A. Kobus, Giordono.

9. Interview, Caggiula.

10. Jung, pp. 40, 41.

11. Interview, Tausig.

12. Interview, A. Kobus.

13. John Hammond Moore, "Getting Fritz to Talk," *Virginia Quarterly Review*, Spring 1978, pp. 265, 273, 274.

14. Interview, A. Kobus.

15. Gansberg, p. 58; interview, A. Kobus.

16. Maj. F. L. Brown, "Memorandum for Chief, Labor and Liaison Branch," Apr. 27, 1945, National Archives, RG 389, PMGO, Box 2514.

17. Interview, Giordono.

18. Lunden, p. 730; Krammer, p. 50.

19. Interview, Wenzel.

20. Letter, H. Wrede to M. Wrede, July 22, 1944.

21. Interview, Tausig.

22. Interviews: Chappell, Wenzel.

23. Interview and diary, E. L.

24. Interview, Gadwah.

25. Interview, Giordono.

26. Interview, E. L.

27. Interviews: Foster, Tausig.

28. John Dvorovy, "Religion in Prisoner of War Camps," *Navy Chaplain*, July-Aug. 1945, p. 17.

29. Letter, Robert Sharp to author, Aug. 4, 1983; interview, Mrs. Robert Sharp, Stark, N.H., Sept. 28, 1986.

30. *Coos County Democrat*, Lancaster, N.H., Oct. 1, 1986, p. 1.

31. Letter, G. Clauss to Raymond White, Oct. 1986.

32. Report of International Red Cross visit (M. Peter), July 24, 1944, National Archives, RG 389, PMGO, Box 2660.

33. Interviews: Tausig, Wenzel, Clauss, Wiemann.

34. Interviews: Giordono, A. Kobus, Wenzel, Wiemann.

35. Interview, Chappell.

36. Interview, Wenzel.

37. Interview, Giordono.

38. Interviews: A. Kobus, Clauss.

39. Interview, A. Kobus.

40. Interview, Clauss.

41. Krammer, p. 63.

42. Interview, Clauss.

43. Interviews: Volz, Tausig.

132 · Notes

44. Letter, H. Wrede to M. Wrede, July 29, 1944.

45. Curt Bondy, "Observation and Re-education of German Prisoners of War," *Harvard Educational Review,* v. 14, Jan., 1944, pp. 12–19; Krammer, pp. 193, 194. Gansberg, *Stalag USA* focuses on the re-education program.

46. Krammer, p. 194.

47. Interview, Ehrmann.

48. Gansberg, pp. 142, 143.

49. Edwin Casady, "The Reorientation Program for PW's at Fort Eustis, Virginia," *The American Oxonian,* July, 1947, pp. 164–154; Q. Reynolds, "Experiment in Democracy," *Colliers,* May 25, 1946, pp. 12, 13, 41, 42.

50. Interview, Foster.

51. Interviews: Clauss, Hoyt, Giordono.

52. Interview, William Joyce quoting Hermann Uelsmann, Stark, N.H., Sept. 28, 1986.

53. Interviews: E. L., Hart.

54. Diary, E. L.

55. Gordon Zahn, *Another Part of the War,* (Amherst: University of Massachusetts Press, 1979), pp. 26, 29; Gordon Zahn, interview, WEVO, Concord, N.H., Jan. 29, 1984; Margaret Landsman-Winer, "Men at Peace," *New Hampshire Times,* Concord, N.H., Jan. 11, 1986, p. 8.

7. Peace and Despair
(pp. 97–107)

1. Interview, Paramas Simonian, Auburn, Mass., June 30, 1986.

2. Interview, Wiemann.

3. Interview, A. Kobus; interview and diary, E. L.

4. Interview, Tausig.

5. Interview, Giordono; Shils and Janowitz, p. 306.

6. Krammer, p. 210; Costelle, p. 205.

7. Pabel, p. 2; Faulk, p. 12.

8. Henry Ehrmann, "An Experience in Political Education," *Social Research,* Sept., 1947, p. 309.

9. Interview, Chappell.

10. Interview, Clauss.

11. Krammer, p. 240.

12. Interviews: A. Kobus, Volz.

13. Böhme, pp. 145, 146; Krammer, p. 240; Moore, "Nazi Troopers in South Carolina," *South Carolina Historical Magazine,* p. 313.

14. Interview and diary, E. L.

15. "Report on IRC Visit to Prisoner of War Camp, Camp Houlton and Branch Camps," May 26, 1945, National Archives, RG 389, PMGO, Box 2664.

16. Interview, A. Kobus.

17. *Newsweek,* May 7, 1945, p. 61; American National Red Cross, "Prisoner of War Bulletin," vol. 3, no. 6, June 1945.

18. Interview, Philip Walton, Stark, N.H., Sept. 28, 1986; *Newsweek,* Apr. 16, 1945, p. 31.

19. Interviews: Clauss, Wiemann; letter, Johann Werner to author, May 27, 1986.
20. Letter, Werner.
21. Letter, Gerhard Clauss to author, Mar. 12, 1985.
22. See also Louis L. Tureen and James O. Palmer, "Some Group Differences in Personal Values Between American Soldiers and German Prisoners of War," Journal of Social Psychology, 42, 1955, pp. 310–312.
23. *Berlin Reporter,* Feb. 7, 1946, p. 1; interviews: Harold Hagar, West Milan, N.H., Jan. 12, 1983; Gadwah, A. Kobus.
24. Interviews: Gadwah, House, Hagar, Clauss.
25. Interview and diary, E. L.; interview, Hagar.
26. *Berlin Reporter,* Jan. 17, 1946, p. 1; interview, A. Kobus.

8. Commencement
(pp. 108–114)

1. Krammer, p. 232.
2. Letter, Lamoureaux, First Service Command, to Brown Co., Nov. 28, 1945.
3. Krammer, p. 233.
4. Krammer, p. 233; report, Abby L. Wilden, U.S. Employment Service, Concord, N.H., Dec. 6, 1945.
5. Krammer, p. 238; telegram, American Pulpwood Association, to Brown Co., Jan. 23, 1946; Lewis and Mewha, p. 173.
6. Interview, E. L.
7. Interviews: Zéler, Volz.
8. Interview, E. L.
9. Interviews: Giordono, A. Kobus.
10. Krammer, p. 266; Lewis and Mewha, p. 20.
11. Interview, Gadwah.
12. R. Billings, unpublished manuscript on German prisoner-of-war attitudes, 1983.
13. Interviews: Clauss, Wiemann, Wenzel, Volz.
14. Interview, House.

9. Auf Wiedersehen
(pp. 115–123)

1. Krammer, p. 254; Lewis and Mewha, p. 263.
2. Report, C. S. Herr, Brown Co., Jan. 29, 1946.
3. Interview, A. Kobus.
4. Davis, p. 630.
5. Interview, Wenzel; *Coos County Democrat,* June 30, 1977, p. 1; *Berlin Reporter,* July 1, 1977, p. 3.

Index

Adams, Sherman, 26
Afrika Korps, 18, 19, 32, 70, 86
Algeria, 18
Alva, Oklahoma, 34
Anti-Nazis, 27, 29, 30, 32, 33, 34, 35, 37, 44, 45, 46, 70, 71, 72, 75, 92, 99, 105
Arizona, 23, 49

Bacher, Franz, 54, 55, 56, 93
Bad Orb, 22, 100
Bavaria, 5, 38
Beattie, Donald, 76
Belgium, 36
Berlin (Germany), 5
Berlin (N.H.), 1, 5, 8, 9, 11, 12, 13, 14, 26, 38, 43, 50, 51, 60, 73, 85, 94, 106, 112, 114
Birmingham (England), 5
Bridges, Styles, 26, 44
Brown Company, 10, 11, 13, 26, 41, 57, 69, 78, 80, 82, 86, 105, 108, 109, 115, 116

Camp Houlton, 98, 109
Chappell, Frank, 65, 88
Christmas, 74, 105
Civilian Conservation Corps, 9, 10, 11, 13, 20, 26, 60, 61, 95
Clauss, Gerhard, 68, 69, 88, 91, 95, 119, 121
Colby-Sawyer College, 117
Croteau, Donald, 79
Croteau, Madeline, 117, 122, 123

Dartmouth College, 119
Death Valley, 22

Dow, Nowak, 106

Easter, 15, 39
Eisenhower, Dwight, 21, 114
Ermarth, Hans Michael, 119

Fort Devens, 27, 34, 37, 45, 47, 54, 69, 83, 98, 106
Fort Eustis, 56, 92, 93, 109
Foster, Elliot, 12, 59, 61, 86, 94, 112

Gadwah, Linwood, 13, 68, 107, 110
Geneva Convention, 16, 17, 20, 21, 22, 23, 24, 25, 44, 48, 50, 60, 82, 83, 87, 92
Georgia, 5
Giordono, Carl, 85
Groveton, 9, 11, 87, 116
Gullion, Allen, 17

Hart, Winston, 112
Heon, Rudolph, 87, 88
Heuberg, 35, 36
Hitler, Adolf, 23, 30, 31, 34, 36, 45, 70, 99
Hoffman, Johann, 52, 53
Hoover, J. Edgar, 48, 49
House, Benny, 62, 112
House, Urania, 112, 114, 117
Hoyt, Warren, 65, 68, 84, 113, 122

International Red Cross, 17, 21, 58, 80, 100

Jaillet, Aquila, 88
Jarclovski, Johann, 59, 93, 94, 113

135

Jurs, August, 112, 114

Kairouan-Pichon, 36
Kiefer, Willi, 79
Kobus, Alexandium, 57, 58, 59, 60,
  61, 69, 80, 81, 82, 87, 88, 99, 100,
  112, 115

Lancaster (N.H.), 32
Lang, Albert, 1, 2, 13, 118
Lang, Hartmut, 120
Leipner, Bruno, 52, 53
Littleton (N.H.), 73
Liverpool, 18

Maine, 5, 44, 46, 57, 98
Mayhew, Lewis, 51
Meuller, Helmut "Red," 81, 86, 110
Miles, Sherman, 60, 82

Nazis, 19, 20, 21, 28, 29, 30, 31, 32,
  33, 34, 35, 36, 37, 44, 45, 46, 48,
  70, 71, 92, 99, 100, 105
New York City, 55
999th Division, 34, 35, 38, 39, 45,
  54, 69, 71, 72, 82, 87, 91, 93, 100
Normandy, 69

Osgood, Electa, 10
Osmer, Herman, 4

Percy (N.H.), 7, 10, 14, 38, 110
Petermann, Albert, 68, 122
Prager, Gerhard, 52
Pusch, Fritz, 53, 54

Renoir, Jean, 95
Revolutionary War, 16, 24

Rhode Island, 92
Richter, Hans, 122
Rief, Roland, 112
Rommel, Erwin, 36, 51
Roosevelt, Franklin, 99

Sarstedt, Johann, 52
Schmurr, Carl, 53, 54
Schwartz, Edgar, 43, 57, 60
Sharp, Robert, 87
Simonian, Bob, 118
Stark, John, 7
Stark, history, 8, 9
Stuttgart, 35

Tatzko, Siegfried, 53, 113
Tausig, Ted, 56, 59, 81, 86, 91, 100
Triebel, Otto, 112
Truman, Harry, 41, 108, 109

Uelsmann, Hermann, 3, 68, 118
Utah, 42

Vancouver, 5
Vermont, 40
Vienna, 5, 56
Volz, Willi, 91

Walton, Phillip, 104
Washington, Mt., 80
Wenzel, Hans, 88
White Mountains, 4, 7, 8, 118
Wiemann, Klauss, 68, 119
World War I, 16, 17, 24
Wyman, David, 104

Y.M.C.A., 17

Zéler, Georges, 85, 91